SO-CEZ-418

BUYING A HOME ON THE INTERNET

Also by CommerceNet Press

Opening Digital Markets: Battle Plans and Business Strategies for Internet Commerce by Walid Mougayar
Understanding Digital Signatures: Establishing Trust over the Internet and Other Networks by Gail Grant
Building Database-Driven Web Catalogs by Sherif Danish and Patrick Gannon
The Search for Digital Excellence by James P. Ware, Judith Gebauer, Amir Hartman, and Malu Roldan
StrikingItRich.com by Jaclyn Easton
How to Invest in E-Commerce Stocks by Bill Burnham and Piper Jaffray

CommerceNet is a nonprofit industry association for companies promoting and building electronic commerce solutions on the Internet. Launched in April 1994 in Silicon Valley, CA, its membership has grown to more than 500 companies and organizations worldwide. They include the leading banks, telecommunications companies, VANs, ISPs, on-line services, software and service companies, as well as end-users, who together are transforming the Internet into a global electronic marketplace. For membership information, please contact CommerceNet at telephone: (650) 858-1930, extension 214; fax: (650) 858-1936; URL: http://www.commerce.net. For information regarding CommerceNet Press, contact Loël McPhee at loel@commerce.net.

BUYING A HOME ON THE INTERNET

ROBERT IRWIN

CommerceNet Press

McGraw-Hill
New York   San Francisco   Washington, D.C.   Auckland   Bogotá
Caracas   Lisbon   London   Madrid   Mexico City   Milan
Montreal   New Delhi   San Juan   Singapore
Sydney   Tokyo   Toronto

Library of Congress Cataloging-in-Publication Data
Applied for.

McGraw-Hill

A Division of The McGraw·Hill Companies

1 2 3 4 5 6 7 8 9 0   DOC/DOC   9 0 3 2 1 0 9 8

ISBN 0-07-134254-0

*The sponsoring editor for this book was Mary Glenn, the editing supervisor was
Tom Laughman, the editing liaison was Patricia V. Amoroso, and the production
supervisor was Pamela A. Pelton. It was set in Times Roman by North Market
Street Graphics.*

Printed and bound by R. R. Donnelley & Sons Company.

McGraw-Hill books are available at special quantity discounts to use as premiums
and sales promotions, or for use in corporate training programs. For more information, please write to the Director of Special Sales, McGraw-Hill, 11 West 19th
Street, New York, NY 10011. Or contact your local bookstore.

CONTENTS

FOREWORD

Let's be honest, using the Internet can be both frustrating and intimidating. There are currently 4.7 million Web sites, and 50,000 new Web sites are being added each week! On the other hand, you've been hearing that the Internet is a great new way to buy, sell, or refinance your home. Everything you've read says that the Internet is making the real estate process easier and saving consumers thousands of dollars in transaction costs.

The problem is that out of the 4.6 million Web sites, you really just want one Web site with that special piece of information, be it the dream home you've been searching for or the cheapest interest rate possible for your mortgage. *Buying a Home on the Internet* not only tells you which of the 4.6 million Web sites are worth visiting, but it goes much further by offering valuable tips on the home-buying process and how to take advantage of the best the Web has to offer.

I know because at E-LOAN, we have invested our future in the Internet. We have transformed our traditional mortgage broker into a company that originates *all* of its business from the Internet. In fact, we are providing over 20,000 rate quotes every day and lending over $1 billion annually. In the process of building E-LOAN, we have observed that the Internet not only makes real estate transactions easier, but the Internet can be one of the most useful tools to do research on all aspects of the transaction. As you read through this book, you will see two recurring themes about how the Internet will help you buy, sell, or refinance a home: (1) the Internet saves time, and (2) the Internet saves money.

THE INTERNET SAVES TIME

The process of buying a home requires many hours focused on weeding out the houses, neighborhoods, and amenities that don't fit your needs or wants. In fact, much of the average buyer's time is spent looking at houses they will not eventually buy. The Internet helps you sort through the real estate market of your choice quickly and in the comfort of your own home or office. Most homes are now listed on the Internet with interior and exterior pictures. It's true, one picture tells a thousand words, and it also saves you wasted drive time by the houses you would never have considered.

Complete information about neighborhoods is also available on-line—how schools rank locally, regionally, and nationally; local crime rates and reports; and other important neighborhood information, such as city government, parks, churches, hospitals, and so forth. Now, you can even get data on all the homes recently sold in a given neighborhood; estimate the value of a home through an on-line, automated appraisal Web site; or, as mentioned before, apply for a loan on-line.

THE INTERNET SAVES MONEY

This is near and dear to most people's hearts. Many real estate companies that use the Internet have found ways to save costs and pass those savings on to the consumer. Even a 0.5-percent price reduction on a sales commission can save hundreds, and sometimes thousands, of dollars. A number of brokers have prenegotiated lower fees for buyers and sellers coming from the Internet. On-line mortgage companies (such as E-LOAN) save up to 75 percent of the fees on either a purchase of a new home or the refinance of your current home.

Today, a thriving on-line real estate industry exists that wasn't even dreamt of just two short years ago. The truth is that, even in its infancy, the Internet is making the home-buying experience easier and more efficient. Thousands are using the Internet every day to conduct real estate transactions, and the number of people visiting real estate Web sites is growing exponentially every month.

Bob Irwin's book is an essential guide to the world of real estate on the Internet because it can effectively direct you through the on-line real estate maze. Enjoy the book and real estate cyberspace.

Doug Galen

PREFACE

Can I *really* buy a home on the Internet?

That's a question I have been asked repeatedly since I began work on this book. Most people are sincerely curious. Can it be done? Will I save time? Money? Will I get a better fit?

The answer is yes, to all. Indeed, I myself recently bought a home I found on the Internet. It is, without question, a home more suited to my needs than any I've ever purchased before (and I've bought a lot of them!). I got it at a bargain price, saved money through on-line mortgage financing, and had a short, smooth escrow. Tens of thousands of others are reporting similar results.

Today, the Internet is the new frontier for home buying. In five years it will be the method of choice. Only you needn't wait five years. I've prepared this book so you can realize the advantages the Web offers home buyers today.

Good Web/house hunting!

www.robertirwin.com

BUYING A HOME ON THE INTERNET

CHAPTER 1

SHOULD I BUY MY HOME ON-LINE?

Should you buy your next home on-line?

Yes, definitely, if you fit one of the following profiles:

- You want to save money on your next home purchase.
- You're being relocated from one part of the country to another, and it's inconvenient to fly to the next location and house hunt.
- You don't have a lot of time to spend looking for a new home.
- You hate being driven around from house to unacceptable house by agents who are constantly pressuring you to buy.
- You want to take advantage of the benefits of electronic purchases.

The Internet and the World Wide Web have changed our lives in so many ways, from buying airline tickets to books, that we're rapidly coming to rely on on-line services for all sorts of purchases. Today you can buy an automobile on-line.

Why not, therefore, purchase your home using the Internet? As you read this there are more than a million homes listed on-line from which you can choose. In fact, there are probably more homes listed for sale on the Internet than not. I recently purchased a home myself and found it using an Internet listing service. The on-line listing contained a full-screen picture of the exterior of the home, and there were additional images of the interior as well as the neighborhood.

As more and more people use the Internet as a source for locating a home, we will increasingly see easily downloadable video that will take us on a virtual tour of homes, walk us around the neighborhood, even introduce us to our next-door neighbors!

Instead of spending countless hours riding around in an agent's car, you can quickly run through available properties that are for sale in the comfort of your computer room. Not only that, you can get prequalified and preapproved for financing and even get your loan funded using on-line services! In short, virtually the entire home-buying process can be shortened, enhanced, and simplified through the use of a computer and on-line services.

Yes, you can buy your next home on-line, and in this book I'll show you exactly how to do it. However, a few caveats are in order. Although you can go through virtually the entire purchase procedure on-line, there are at least three times that I recommend you don't. The first is after you've located your potential purchase. Before signing the actual sales agreement, I suggest you go to the property and look it and the neighborhood over. I'll explain why in Chapter 4. The second is when you accompany the inspector to physically check it out. We'll see why you should do this in Chapter 9. The last is when you sign your closing documents. At the present time, you'll need to go to a physical location, and you should have a legal advisor with you. (In the future as on-line security and verification procedures get better, you will probably be able to eliminate this step.)

DO I HAVE TO BE "COMPUTER SAVVY" TO DO IT?

Heavens, no!

But you do need a computer with a modem and a phone line. Your expertise in running the computer is limited only to being able to get connected to a provider, such as America Online, Microsoft Network, CompuServe Corporation, Prodigy, AT&T's WorldNet Service, Earthlink, or any of dozens of others and then being able to search the Internet (which we'll go into in detail in the next chapter).

An estimated 30 to 50 million people already are doing this and if you're one of these, you know exactly what I'm talking about. On the other hand, if you haven't yet entered the world of connectivity that the Internet offers, here's exactly how to get started.

Step 1. Get a computer (or one of the WebTV access devices that connects to your television set). The computer does not have to be particularly fast, powerful, or expensive. Rather than go into specific details, because computers advance so rapidly, let's just say if your computer is a year old or less and has a modem, it should work fine. Of course, the faster the modem (which is what connects to the phone line) you have, the easier will be your home search.

Step 2. Get an Internet service provider (ISP). The numbers for a half dozen of the top services are listed in the next chapter. They will connect you to the Internet for a fee, typically around $20 a month. They will also provide you with all the software you need to make the connection (and virtually all will provide you with e-mail, which is one of the Internet's best services).

Step 3. Find a house and buy it! In effect, the rest of this book is step 3. The first two steps are incredibly easy and so is the third. I'm just here to help provide a bit of guidance and a few suggestions regarding real estate to see that you don't make a misstep or fall into a trap that could cost you time, money, and headache.

HINT

At least one Internet mortgage service, eloan.com, is providing free computers to those with low incomes in poor economic areas to help them get connected. It is being done in conjunction with the National Urban League and Black Homes On-Line (blackhomes.com).

So, let's get started. If you already are preapproved for a mortgage and know how much you can get, move right along to the next chapter. There we'll see how to locate the home of your dreams. On the other hand, if you're not sure about how much you can finance, you may want to skip ahead to Chapter 7 where we learn about mortgages and how large an amount you can get.

2 CHAPTER

HOW DO I FIND HOME LISTINGS ON-LINE?

Making the decision to shop for a home electronically means you've chosen the most efficient method of property location ever to be developed. You're on the real estate forefront, and your choice should allow you to be more informed, save time, and most important, get the best deal.

Of course, you're not alone. Real estate agents have been using electronic home searches for years. Drop into a modern office and the first thing an agent is likely to do (after introductions, of course, and some basic questions to ask what you're looking for) is plop you down in front of a computer monitor that begins spilling out all of the homes listed in your price range. In an electronically savvy office, as soon as you pick out a home you think you might be interested in, it'll be shown to you as a color picture on-screen, and its highlights will be spit out by the computer's printer.

That's handy, *if* you're sure you're with the right agent, in the right part of town (in the right community), and don't mind running around to see the homes this particular agent wants to show you.

However, while you may still want to deal with an agent to make the purchase (unless you want to buy directly from a seller, discussed shortly), there's no longer any reason you must sit with that agent to search for the home electronically. All you need is your own computer, a modem, and an

5

Internet provider. You can log on and check out virtually all of the homes the agent can show you . . . and chances are, far more!

HOW DO I GET CONNECTED?

How do I access the homes listed on the Web? For those who are Web experienced, this may seem like a simple-minded question. But actually, it's not. Everyone has to learn the first time, and if it's all new to you, it can seem a great mystery. Actually, however, it's quite easy.

I'm going to presume you have a provider. If not, you can easily get one. Most new computers come loaded with the software to automatically connect you to such providers as:

America Online (AOL)   (800) 827-6364
Microsoft Network (MSN)   (800) 373-3676
Earthlink Network   (800) 395-8410
CompuServe (CSI)   (800) 368-3343
AT&T WorldNet   (800) 400-1447
Prodigy   (800) 213-0992

And there is a host of others. If for some reason you don't have access to these services already programmed right into your computer, you can call the above numbers and receive the software and instructions to get started. The cost to sign up is minimal, and most charge around $20 a month, as of this writing, for virtually unlimited Internet access.

HOW DO I FIND A REAL ESTATE WEB SITE?

Once you have a provider, the question becomes, how do you access the Internet directly and get to a real estate Web site?

It couldn't be easier. Once you log onto your provider (and it will give you instructions telling you exactly how), it will usually take you to its own Web site, where it will spend a lot of time promoting itself, including advertisements. (Don't knock them, they help pay the bill so your charges are smaller.)

Your provider may have a button or arrow that will direct you to the Internet. Or you may need to use a keyword such as "Internet" to get there.

As soon as you push the appropriate button or type the keyword, you'll be connected by either Microsoft's Internet Explorer or Netscape's browser. (You may already be using one of these to access your provider.)

These are the two main browsers for swimming in the Internet and, truth be told, there's not much difference between them.

What you are looking for is an address line that will, typically, have the provider's own screen address on it. For example, at AOL the address might be http://www.aol.com. For MSN it might be http://www.msn.com.

Now, use your mouse to highlight the address shown. Once it's highlighted, simply write in the new address you want to go to (assuming you know where you want to go). For example, you might type in http://www .owners.com. Now press ENTER and the miracle of Internet electronics will take you to that Web site.

WHAT DO I DO ONCE I GET TO A REAL ESTATE WEB SITE?

Investigate. Use your cursor to highlight certain hot spots or hot buttons that appear on the page. These will take you to other pages on the site that provide more detailed information. Use the BACK or FORWARD of your browser to move between the pages.

Very quickly you'll discover all that there is to know about the site. You'll also be able to move to descriptions of properties and then onto individual listings, which we'll cover shortly.

WHAT IF I DON'T KNOW THE SCREEN ADDRESS?

That's also easy. There are at least a dozen search engines on the Web that, for no fee at all, will search for real estate Web sites. Just go to their Web site and use their free search capabilities. (I'll suggest search words to use, shortly.) Some of the best search engines for real estate include:

www.yahoo.com

www.excite.com

www.lycos.com

www.infoseek.com

www.altavista.com

and more (see Figure 2.1).

In addition, there may be a Web search engine built right into your provider, such as NetFind with AOL. However, no matter which engine you use, you will probably end up using several others as well. The Web is so enormous and so complex that even the best providers may actually end

FIGURE 2.1

Yahoo! opening page.

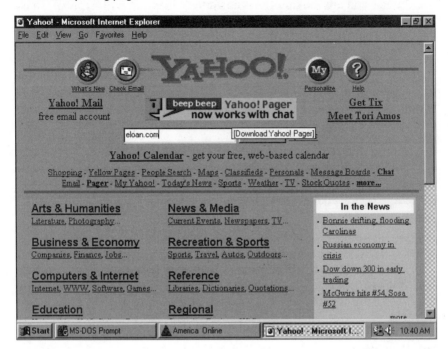

up searching only a tiny percentage of it. Using several search engines will help expand your opportunities for finding just the site you want. Furthermore, many of the search engines also include real estate listings (such as Infoseek, Yahoo!, and others).

My suggestion is that once you get to a search engine, you type in the following keywords, which will help that engine reveal new sites you will want to explore. The best keywords for real estate listings are:

real estate

real estate listings

real estate for sale

homes

homes for sale

FSBO

by owner real estate

These should get you started and quickly send you to a wide variety of good Web sites.

ARE THERE LOTS OF HOME SALES SITES ON THE INTERNET?

When I began writing this book, there were only a couple of really good sites for locating a home on the Internet. However, during the course of writing the book, a whole host of new Web sites appeared; today, there are literally thousands. Apparently the competition is heating up to list properties electronically as real estate agents begin to realize that this is how most people in the future will look for property.

realtor.com

This is the granddaddy of listing sites. This service is operated by Real Select, Inc., in Los Angeles, in cooperation with the National Association of Realtors ©.

As of this writing, this site, which has been around for years, has over a million listings taken from Realtor's Multiple Listing boards around the country. In a great many cases, much of the same information that you can get by checking with a broker on his or her office computer, you can obtain yourself using your own computer, in your own home, over the Internet at this address.

In addition, well established on the Web are the following sites, which you will likewise want to check out.

Cyber homes.com

This service, as do others, begins with a map and then works its way down to the street level in those communities that it covers. It also offers homes from the MLS (agent-operated Multiple Listing Service). And it provides information from national, state, and local school records using a service called "School Match." Basic information is provided free with detailed information on specific schools and districts available for a fee. I was able to locate individual schools in my neighborhood using this service and get detailed information on them.

Homes.com

This site is connected with *Homes and Land Magazine,* which is distributed free, and it lists homes for sale as well as apartment and condo rentals.

It begins with a U.S. map, which then leads you to a state map, which lists the communities in which homes are listed. I found the site to have many homes in some areas and few to none in others. The listings are from real estate agents, and often there are links to the broker's office's own Web sites as well as other properties by the listing agent.

homescout.com

This service is operated by homeshark.com, which offers mortgages on-line. (More about homeshark.com in Chapter 7.) Homescout is a service that checks other services. As of this writing, it claims it will search 350 other on-line listing services to come up with homes for you by location, price, and other categories such as number of bedrooms. I have found that it can usually produce listings for almost any location where I wanted to look. Certainly a must resource for the home hunter.

HomeAdvisor.com

Much more recently, a new Web site has appeared, sponsored in part by Microsoft. This site also includes hundreds of thousands of listings compiled from the MLS of brokers around the country. In addition, its graphics are spiffy, and as with most of the other sites, it includes geographical maps and, with a twist, an integrated mortgage finance component. (The other sites often include a hot link to mortgage finance sites.)

More to the point, it also says it will provide information on neighborhoods. This would include school comparative test results and crime statistics. A real boon to home searchers.

HomeAdvisor has apparently offered to pay agents who list on their site. As a result, the other listing services may begin paying as well. On the surface this means only better service for you, the consumer. You're likely to get more homes listed and have a bigger selection.

However, there is also the possibility of exclusivity. One site may say that they will only carry and pay for a listing if it is exclusively listed there. As a result, instead of homes being listed on multiple sites, they will only be listed on one, and you'll have to check each site to not overlook any homes.

WHAT ABOUT FSBOs?

FSBO stands for "For Sale by Owner." Thus far, the sites we've been discussing offer properties listed by agents. But the Internet offers enormous possibilities for home sellers to promote their own properties. There are many FSBO sites.

owners.com

This is a growing Web site that offers strictly FSBO listings. It does, however, have a few additional plusses. For example, it offers audio downloads of current information. When I visited most recently I was able to download a five-minute portion of a public radio broadcast talking about owners.com and FSBOs versus listed properties in general.

It also has a sophisticated link to a mortgage page that will help to quickly get up to speed on how much financing you can afford. (We'll have much more to say about electronic financing in a later chapter.)

yahoo.com

The granddaddy of search engines also offers its own listing sheet on which FSBOs can put up their homes for sale. The site is extensive with listings from across the country. This is a site you won't want to miss out on. However, as of this writing, it does not include photos of the subject properties. However, many listers will link to their own home pages where they do have photos available.

Of course, we've barely scratched the surface. There are dozens, perhaps thousands, of other services for both agent-listed and FSBO properties. To see what's current when you search, check out the search engines noted earlier.

3
CHAPTER

HOW DO I FIND THE HOME I WANT ON-LINE?

If you've read Chapter 2 and have gone on-line to see what's available, you'll quickly realize that the issue is not one of a scarcity of homes for sale, but rather one of overabundance. How do you choose which homes might be right for you out of the thousands available? How do you narrow your search, eventually down to that one home that you'll want to buy?

In this chapter, we're going to see how to begin with just a general picture of what you want in a home and then narrow that down to just a couple of homes in specific neighborhoods. Along the way, we'll learn what's important and what's not when house hunting on the Internet.

WHAT'S THE MOST IMPORTANT CONSIDERATION?

It's been said ad nauseam, but it remains a constant truth: "In real estate the most important consideration is location." Whether you buy the old-fashioned way or on-line, where you buy will be the single biggest determiner of both how well you enjoy your home and how profitable it will prove to be.

Buy in a location close to work, schools, shopping, hospitals and doctors, even recreational facilities, and no matter what your needs or desires, you'll find them quickly and easily met. That is to say, you'll enjoy living there.

Further, buy in an area that others find desirable (often for the very factors noted above), and you'll notice rapid and constant price appreciation that will make you very happy when it's time to sell.

On the other hand, buy badly, and you'll regret your tenure of ownership and regret it even more when you try to resell.

HOW DO I FIND A GOOD LOCATION WHEN BUYING ON-LINE?

Finding a good location for a home when purchasing on-line presents both special advantages as well as distinct drawbacks. Perhaps the best way of approaching the whole issue of finding the good location on-line is to compare it with doing it the old-fashioned way, on foot.

If you had never seen a computer or heard of the Internet and you wanted to buy a home, the first thing you would probably do is to pick a general location. Unless you already have a specific area in mind (see a later section), this most often depends on where you work. Most people must live close to their jobs. Of course, if you're retired or have some other consideration, then that will determine the specific location you want to be near.

If your job is in Seattle, for example, it's unlikely you'll want to live in Portland. If you're working in New York, Philadelphia might be a bit far to commute. You want to live within a reasonably close distance to work.

How close? That depends on your expectations. On the east coast a commute of an hour or less is usually considered reasonable. On the west coast, that frequently jumps to two hours or more.

Don't Confuse Distance with Time

Note that commuting distance is usually measured in time, not miles. It really doesn't matter how far away your home is from work; what matters is how long it takes to get there. In certain parts of the Silicon Valley (San Jose, California), during peak rush hour periods, it can take upward of an hour or more to commute less than five miles. On the other hand, on open freeways/turnpikes, you might travel sixty to seventy miles within the same time frame.

Thus, how far away you will be willing to live from your work will depend on how long you're willing to commute and how crowded the area is. When attempting to find an area in which to look, it's important to judge commute *time*.

If you're physically going out to look for a home, this often becomes a matter of trial and error. You'll go out on one roadway during peak hours and see how long it takes to go what you consider a reasonable commuting distance (say 45 minutes). You might try the same thing using mass transit (of course, allowing for time to get to the train or bus station, park the car, and then from the terminal to work). By going in various directions and by experimentation, you could get a map of the overall area and draw circles around communities adjacent to roadways, railways, bus lines, and so forth that were within commuting distance. It might take you a few weeks to accomplish, but if you dogged it out and were precise, you could get a very accurate reading of what communities were available to you.

But, how do you accomplish this if you're buying on-line?

HOW CAN I NARROW DOWN MY GEOGRAPHICAL SEARCH ON-LINE?

At first, one might think that it would be virtually impossible to do the same thing on-line as I just described doing physically. Actually, the opposite is true. It's far easier on-line. You can let your fingers and keyboard do the searching that you otherwise would do on foot.

Virtually all on-line listing services provide maps. These maps can be very general, covering a large area. They can also be very detailed, in some cases right down to individual streets, cul-de-sacs, and so forth. Thus, by availing yourself of the maps provided with on-line listing services, you can

HINT

To find maps of any area of the country, go to virtually any search engine and use the keyword "maps" + the area you want. Most search engines provide you with maps of most cities. In addition, you'll be astonished at how many sites provide good maps for you. If you're a member of AAA (American Automobile Associations), their Route Master® can provide detailed maps of almost any location in the country.
www.aaa.com
www.maps.com

HINT

Many map sites ask you for a specific address. You may want to get a street address near where you're looking first to help in your search.

quickly pinpoint where you will be working and then see the roadways and, sometimes, the mass transit lines that connect to it. In other words, you have an on-line map to guide you. Of course, while this will tell you what's geographically near your work, it won't help much with commute times. (However, I understand some listing services are going to be providing that as well.) (See Figure 3.1.)

How Do I Find Out Commute Times On-Line?

Finding commute times, however, can be a bit trickier. Arbitrarily pick a community that looks as though it might be within reasonable commuting

FIGURE 3.1

Map from owners.com listing site.

Buying a Home on the Internet

distance. Then use the site locating service to call up homes listed in the area. Once you're at the level of individual listings, pick a couple that are in your price range and that look interesting. Then contact the agents by e-mail. Simply explain that you're trying to find out how far, in time, it would take to commute from the listing to work. Ask for a quick reply.

HOW DO I CHECK OUT THE COMMUNITIES?

Once you've narrowed your search down to communities that might be acceptable in terms of commute times, it's now important to examine the various cities or communities themselves. Perhaps your initial search has led you to a dozen or more different possibilities. What do you know about them? They might be just what you're looking for. Or they could be for the super wealthy and far beyond your means. Or they could be filled with blighted areas where you'd never want to live. How do you narrow your search down further.

If you didn't have a computer, modem, and the Internet, you'd hop into your trusty jalopy and drive over to see them. You might spend a day or more in each looking them over, perhaps stopping by the Chamber of Commerce, maybe dropping into an agent to see a few houses. Your search, if thorough (which most people's were not), could take weeks or a month or more.

But, you are set up on-line. So what you do is go to one of the major search engines and you type in the name of the community, city, or even neighborhood (if you've identified one or more). Very likely

HINT

A very astute member of Congress once commented that all politics is local. Interestingly enough, the same applies to real estate. Over and again in this book we'll emphasize that good agents know a small, restricted geographical area, but they know it very, very well. If you ask them how long it takes to commute from their community to a nearby town, they can usually give you that information off the top of their heads. Ask two agents and get the same answer and you've got a reliable fact.

WARNING

While virtually all communities will have a Web site, not all sites will be equally well created or maintained. A terrific community may simply not have the energy, talent, or desire to spend the funds to put up a super Web presence. On the other hand, a slum may put up a terrific Web site in the hope of attracting interest. You have to look beyond the snazzy appearance, the color, and the visuals to the facts themselves.

you'll find one or more Web sites for each area. Today, virtually every city, community, and organized neighborhood has a Web presence. You don't have to go there to find out about it . . . you just have to point and click.

Now simply go to the site and check it out. Communities will typically show you pictures of some of their more prominent areas. They will also have all sorts of facts and statistics. From the city or community's Web site you should be able to learn the following, all without leaving your computer room:

Community size and population
Major industries and businesses
Demographics
Location of parks and other recreational facilities
Maps showing specific neighborhoods and direction of growth
Religious facilities, including temples and churches
Newspapers and magazines published in the area (which you may want to send for a sample issue)
Sports teams, hotels, restaurants, and medical facilities
Other factors the community may be proud of, such as
strict zoning controls, slow growth, and so on

Some communities will sound wonderful, and you'll feel that they could make a real home for you. Others will simply not be your style, and you'll probably shy away from them. Either way, however, you should very quickly be able to limit your search down to only three or four choices.

FIGURE 3.2

San Francisco Chamber of Commerce Web site.

Here are some typical Chamber of Commerce screen addresses:

www.sfchamber.com   San Francisco, California, Chamber of Commerce (see Figure 3.2)

www.seattlechamber.com   Seattle, Washington, Chamber of Commerce

www.orlando.org   Greater Orlando, Florida, Chamber of Commerce

Check Out Real Estate Boards

Check out the local real estate board. Most boards now maintain their own Web sites and will have specific information on homes. From the real estate board's Web site you may be able to glean valuable information. Many will offer listings and lists of members. But some will also offer:

Average and median price for homes sold by neighborhood and by area

HINT

The more homes listed and the longer the time it takes to sell, the slower the market. The fewer homes listed and the shorter the time it takes to sell, the hotter the market.

Number of homes currently listed and whether that number is higher or lower than normal
The number of days until a listed home sells

This information will help you to quickly determine whether the market in the area is hot, cold, or just simmering.

Look for average and median home prices, number of parks, demographics, and so on. Many sites will offer to send or e-mail you additional information on the community. Request this. The more information you gather about a community, the more you will be able to judge whether you want to live there. This type of search is often more thorough and revealing than doing it the old-fashioned way, by just driving down a few streets to see whether you like the feel of the place.

To find these addresses, search under Board of Realtors. Some sample addresses are:

www.avbor.com Antelope Valley, California, Board of Realtors

www.mibor.com Metropolitan Indianapolis, Indiana, Board of Realtors (Figure 3.3)

www.newquestcity.com/al/board.htm Calhoun County, Alabama, Board of Realtors

What About Crime Statistics?

Like it or not, we live in an age when crime is a major factor in our lives. We all want to live in a low-crime area. When we buy we are well advised to check out the crime rate in the area.

Local crime statistics are available from police departments. They are available by communities as a whole, by neighborhoods, and even by blocks within a neighborhood. Some police departments maintain Web sites, but many don't. To find information on the Internet, search for keywords "crime enforcement" and "crime prevention."

FIGURE 3.3

Metropolitan Indianapolis Board of Realtors Web site.

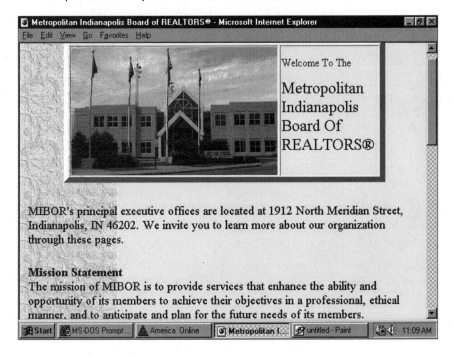

For those police departments that don't have a Web site, you may have to invest in a phone call. Ask to speak to the community relations officer. The name will vary by police department, but in almost all cases a person will have a similar title and will be happy to help you. Just ask for the number of murders, robberies, muggings, rapes, or whatever has been *reported* in a specific area within the past six months to a year. This is public information and it will be quickly given to you. You can very quickly learn how bad, or good, the community you are considering is.

Here are a few typical police department screen addresses:

www.santamonicapd.org   Santa Monica, California, Police

www.ci.boston.ma.us/bpdtemp/index.htm   Boston, Massachusetts, Police (Figure 3.4)

www.ci.dallas.tx.us/dpd   Dallas, Texas, Police

FIGURE 3.4

Boston Police Department home page.

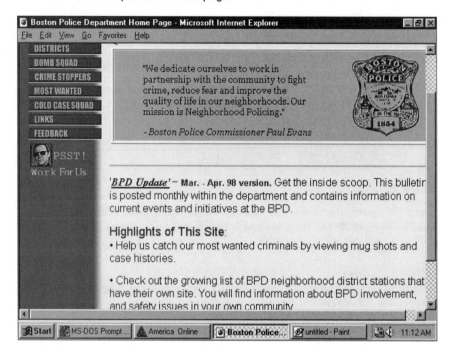

What About Schools?

Perhaps the single most important factor to many people when buying homes is the quality of the local schools. Indeed, it almost goes without saying that in real estate, those areas with good schools see rapid price appreciation, whereas those with bad see home prices stagnate or even go down.

You will want to check out the schools in the neighborhoods you are considering. Most school districts now have their own Web sites. They often will give scholastic scores on national and state tests by district, by school, and even by grade level. These scores compare how well the local school did with national (or state) norms. You may be able to see whether the school in which your children will go (information which should be supplied on the listing or by the agent) compares with others. If it's in the 80th percentile, it suggests one thing. If it's in the 20th, it suggests another.

Homefair offers data on a variety of subjects, including the locaiton of schools within a district, district comparisons within a county, availability of child care, as well as the teacher-student ratio and average class sizes. If you submit your name and personal data, it can have a report sent to you on a specific school.

Global SchoolNet has links to thousands of individual schools around the country that have their own Web site. You can quickly tap into the school you're interested in and get some very local information.

www.homefair.com
www.gsn.org/hotlist/index.html
(Global SchoolNet)

HOW DO I NARROW MY SEARCH FURTHER AFTER I KNOW THE AREA?

Once you know the community(ies) in which you most likely will want to purchase your home, there's the matter of picking the neighborhood. If we weren't constricted by price, home size, and desired amenities, we could simply pick any neighborhood at all. However, in real life, we can only live where we can afford to buy the type and size of home we need and want. Therefore, once you narrow your search down to the point at which you're considering neighborhoods, my suggestion is that you switch your approach.

Now begin searching for homes by price, size, number of bedrooms, and amenities you must have. Most listing sites make this kind of search quite easy as they have built-in locators that do the work for you.

Typically, you'll be asked for a price range (all homes in the area between a bottom and top price or all homes below a certain price), the square footage, number of bedrooms, and the number of baths. These four represent the most elemental factors in differentiating between homes:

HINT

For those who are dedicated to doing everything on the Web, I am aware that there are organizations that put crime statistics up on various sites. However, I'm never really comfortable with these as, except in the case of federal crimes, they tend to be gleaned secondhand. I think you're far better off to check individually with the local departments. Besides, by looking at a police department's Web site or by talking with an officer, you can often learn a lot more information in between the lines.

Price

Square footage

Bedrooms

Baths

How do you know what price, square footage, bedrooms, and baths you need, want, and can likely afford (see Figure 3.5)?

How Do I Know What Price I Can Afford?

This is usually a matter of financing. The question often is not really how much can I afford, but how much can I finance? In the juggling act of buying a home, it's just another ball you need to keep in the air.

If you already know what you can afford/finance, then you can proceed to enter that data in the listing sites locator. If you don't, then you may want to turn to Chapter 7, which will help you come up with that information.

FIGURE 3.5

Typical listing site.

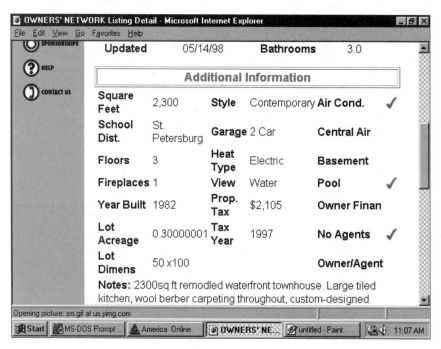

How Big a House Should I Look For?

This is a case in which bigger is better. I can recall a time only a few years ago, when the futurists were predicting that as the baby boomers aged and their kids left home, they'd be downsizing. As a result, smaller homes would become more desirable.

The logic is irrefutable. Unfortunately, like those philosophers who sat in their corners trying to logically determine how many angels could dance on the head of a pin, it's also somewhat irrelevant. What has happened is that as the population has aged and as children have left the baby boomers, the parents have opted for a different kind of house, not necessarily a smaller one. Older Americans still want space, lots of it. They just don't want as many bedrooms. Instead of a home with five cramped bedrooms, they'd prefer three larger ones—a master bedroom, a room for an office, and a guest room, and a nice, large den/family room, living room, and particularly, a large kitchen with an eating area in it.

It seems that regardless of age or need, Americans like large homes. Thus, homes that have 2000 square feet or more tend to sell better than those that are smaller.

This holds true whether you're looking for single-family homes, condos, town homes, or whatever. (Check into Chapter 11 for more info on communal-style homes.) The more room to roam, the more likely you will be to enjoy the home and make a bigger profit on it when you sell.

Therefore, when a listing site asks for square footage, I always suggest putting in at least 2000 square feet as a minimum. You can always downsize to a smaller home *if* you find there's nothing in your price range at that size. However, if you can afford it, you're probably better off buying bigger.

How Many Bedrooms Should I Seek?

Avoid homes with only two bedrooms. Three or four are considered the easiest to resell. Avoid homes with five or more bedrooms, unless the home is very large and, consequently, can adequately handle more bedrooms. If you want a home with five bedrooms, you'll probably want 2400 square feet or larger (see Figure 3.6).

The ideal home remains one with three bedrooms and a den. Typically the den is convertible. You can use it as a study, or you can convert it to a bedroom should you have additional guests. This flexibility makes it

FIGURE 3.6

Home locator.

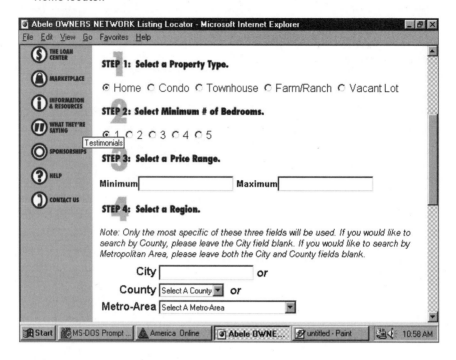

highly desirable. Straight four-bedroom homes are less desirable than three and a den.

For a time a number of homes with only two bedrooms, both master suites, were built in various locations around the country. These got lots of attention in newspapers and magazines as the "home of the future" for empty nesters (those whose kids had grown up and left). The couple slept in one master suite, whereas the other was for guests.

However, it only seems to work out if there's actually a third bedroom/den. In those cases in which there were truly only two bedrooms, reselling becomes tricky. I would not want to buy a home with only two bedrooms unless I planned to remodel and add a third.

How Many Bathrooms Should I Look For?

Never buy a home with only one bath, unless you intend to remodel and add another. You won't like it while you live there, particularly if you have children. It always seems to be the case that just when one person needs to use it, another needs to use it as well.

These days, homes with three bathrooms, or at least two and a "half" or two and "three-quarters" (as agents refer to them), should be considered a minimum. By the way, a half bath means that there's only a toilet and a sink, whereas three-quarters means a toilet, sink, and shower. A full bath is a toilet, sink, shower, and tub. Typically the bathrooms are arranged as follows: one is in the master bedroom, another is adjacent to the remaining bedrooms, and the smallest is usually located near the living/family/kitchen area for guests.

I recently bought a home with only two baths, and I know the fact that it doesn't have the third will make it somewhat harder to sell. However, homes with at least two baths will work for many families. And if the price, location, and other amenities are what you want, then perhaps two will do.

Some homes have more baths than you need. I once owned a home with six bathrooms. It was ridiculous. The work and expense of just keeping them clean made them undesirable. Ultimately, we closed off three of them that we almost never used. If you're wealthy and can afford opulence, then by all means be extravagant and have a half-dozen baths or more. For the rest of us, two or three will do nicely.

WHAT INFO TO ENTER?

Unless you have specific parameters, once you get the neighborhood or community defined, I would suggest you give the following general parameters:

Price Determine the price you can afford from Chapter 7, then add 5 or 10 percent. Remember, except in very hot markets, you'll pay less than the asking price. Therefore, you want to look for homes higher than you think you can afford. Also, you might find a home you really like that's just a bit more than you think you can afford and you may want to stretch to get it.

Size If you're given this option, simply enter 2000 square feet, unless you're looking specifically for a bigger or smaller home.

Bedrooms Enter three or four, again unless you have a reason for wanting more. I wouldn't suggest getting a home with less.

Baths If you're given this option, enter two or three. You just don't want a home with only one.

See Figure 3.7 for a list of homes, the result of an on-line search.

FIGURE 3.7

List of homes—the result of an on-line search.

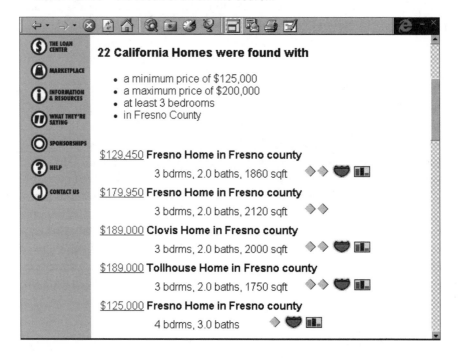

HOW DO I PICK FROM THE LIST I'M GIVEN?

If you've logged onto a good listing site, one with a great many thousands of homes, there should be quite a few in your area, price range, size, bedrooms, and baths. Let's say you use the locator and find out there are fourteen homes roughly fitting your parameters within the community you've selected. Now what do you do? How do you continue to narrow the search to find just the right home for you?

Check Out Each of the Photos

Hopefully, there'll be a picture showing at least one view (usually the front) of the home. It's been said often enough that a picture is worth a thousand words. However, sometimes, particularly when the desire is to make the home seem grander or prettier than it really is, the picture can be deceptive. Nevertheless, it's a good place to start. Scan through the listings just looking at the pictures. You're not trying to find the perfect home this way; rather, you're trying to eliminate those you simply wouldn't be interested in.

For example, you may be interested in a Tudor-style home, and thirteen out of the fourteen you've selected are western, split-level ranch homes. You've quickly narrowed your search (or been forced to enlarge your requirements!).

Or, you don't want a big driveway in front or a lot of lawn area, and half of the homes have this undesirable (for you) feature. Again, you can eliminate them. Use the photos to good advantage. Although they may not show you what you want, they often show you what you don't want.

Check Out the Expanded Information

Usually, once you're at the level of individual listings, there is much more information posted that you can check out. For example, here's a short list of items that might be included, which will help you make up your mind about the home. Note: it's unlikely that any one site would include all of this information. But many sites will have most of it. Choose here what you want.

Size of lot? _____ sq ft

Size of home? _____ sq ft

On sewer?	Yes ☐	No ☐
On septic systems?	Yes ☐	No ☐
Family room included?	Yes ☐	No ☐
Den included?	Yes ☐	No ☐
Washer/dryer room inside?	Yes ☐	No ☐
Washer/dryer in garage?	Yes ☐	No ☐
One- ☐, two- ☐, three- ☐ car garage?		
Pool?	Yes ☐	No ☐
Spa?	Yes ☐	No ☐
Cement patio?	Yes ☐	No ☐
Two stories?	Yes ☐	No ☐
Playroom in basement?	Yes ☐	No ☐
Stucco exterior?	Yes ☐	No ☐
Wood exterior?	Yes ☐	No ☐
Siding on exterior?	Yes ☐	No ☐

Vaulted ceilings?	Yes ☐	No ☐
Skylights?	Yes ☐	No ☐
Trash compactor in kitchen?	Yes ☐	No ☐
Dishwasher in kitchen?	Yes ☐	No ☐
Sub-zero refrigerator?	Yes ☐	No ☐
Island in kitchen?	Yes ☐	No ☐
Room for RV on side?	Yes ☐	No ☐
HOA (Home Owner's Association)?	Yes ☐	No ☐
Strictly enforced CC&Rs?	Yes ☐	No ☐

The list can be much longer or shorter. It might have different items. But much can be gleaned from it. For example, you would expect to have a dishwasher in the kitchen. Not having one would say mountains about the quality of construction. On the other hand, only better-quality homes, typically custom- rather than tract-built, have trash compactors and islands in the kitchen.

Having room for an RV on the side of the house indicates an area that allows you to park RVs, and it may be just the choice for a more adventuresome buyer who wants a less-restricted lifestyle than you're likely to find in highly regulated developments.

A close reading of the additional information may help you to further narrow your search. If you start out with a dozen possible target homes, after looking at the picture and carefully reading the additional information, you may end up with only seven or eight to choose from in a particular area.

WHAT IF I'VE EXHAUSTED ALL THE INFORMATION GIVEN WITH THE LISTING?

It's time to ask for more. Contact the listing agent or the seller (if it's by FSBO). Usually you can do this by e-mail, often directly from the listing site. Sometimes, it will be necessary to make a phone call or to fax.

Explain that you are seriously interested in purchasing a home, that you like the community, and from what you see of the listing, you like the property. Only you want more information before you can make any kind of a decision. The information you ask for should include:

Additional photos (or a videotape, if available) showing the interior, the exterior, and views of the neighborhood

Information on the HOA including whether there are any community meetings (such as potluck dinners, newcomers' groups, and so on) and whether there are recreational facilities (such as community pools, spas, and rec areas)

History of the home itself how long the sellers have been there, why they are moving (this information may not be reliable), any problems with the home (required in most states under disclosures), and so on

Sense of the neighborhood lots of children; mostly older, retired people; sense of community

It's positively amazing how much information you can get, if only you ask for it specifically. Agents are usually most helpful because they have anticipated most of your questions and will be ready with answers. Owners selling by themselves may not know all the information and may need time to gather it. On the other hand, owners/ sellers may be far more forthcoming on their true reasons for selling and their forthright evaluation of neighbors and the area.

IN WHAT FORM IS THE INFORMATION LIKELY TO BE?

It's important to realize that as far as the Internet and information on housing have come, they still have a long way to go. Some listers may be fully prepared to give you everything electronically. A well-setup real estate office or fully prepared FSBO, for

HINT
Many areas, even with single-family homes, have home owner's associations and highly restrictive covenants, conditions, and restrictions (CC&Rs) written into the deed of each home in the area. These often restrict the landscaping you must have, the color you may paint your home, any additions or external remodeling you may do, even the kind of mailbox you may have in front! Although many people balk at living under such restrictions, others like it because it guarantees a minimum quality to the neighborhood.

example, may be able to upload a dozen different still photos for you to see. In addition, they may have toured the home and neighborhood with a camcorder and recorded fifteen or twenty minutes of video and audio. They can easily upload this to a variety of sites on the Internet ready to handle it, and you can download it as "streaming video" to your computer, usually without the need for any additional software. (You download the needed playback software in addition to the video.)

As of this writing, however, this tends to be far and away the exception rather than the rule. Although in the near future multiple photos scanned (digitized) and put on the Web site and full-size, downloaded videos may become common, today it is more than likely that you're going to get a series of photos sent to you by snail mail (the U.S. Post Office). And, if you're very lucky, a VHS video may be included as well.

Of course, any written information can much more easily be transmitted by e-mail.

Look at what you get. Most certainly it will narrow your search even further. Indeed, after talking with the lister and/or seller, getting additional photos/video and written information, you may narrow your search down to two or three homes within a neighborhood, and perhaps two or three neighborhoods—in other words, about half a dozen houses. If you're very careful, you may, in fact, have narrowed your search down to one or two homes.

IS IT TIME TO VISIT THE HOMES?

Consider what you've accomplished. Sitting at home in your computer room in a matter of hours (if you're lucky) or within a few days, you could have searched part of an entire state for every home listed electronically (which currently includes most homes listed and soon will include nearly all of them), searched by city, community, and neighborhood, and found out what you need to know about:

Crime
Housing market and prices
HOAs
Types of homes
Educational facilities
Size, bedrooms, baths, and full descriptions including photos of homes you might be interested in

You have found out virtually everything else you could possibly want to know about the area, the neighborhood, and the house you are considering. And you've done it all without leaving your computer room. You haven't been dragged around by an agent. You haven't become exhausted

HINT

All real estate is unique.

looking at dozens of homes you're not interested in. You haven't spent very much time, really, at all.

But, now that's going to change. Now that you've isolated the few properties that you're really interested in, you've got to get off your duff and actually go down and see them.

Why? I'm sure many a computer maven is wondering why bother? Why can't we make the choice electronically?

ALL REAL ESTATE IS UNIQUE

It's time for the last rule in this chapter.

Unlike jars of mayonnaise or television sets or even automobiles, each individual unit in real estate is unique. Even seemingly identical houses in a tract are unique in the way they are constructed, how they are placed on their lots, how their lots approach the street and other homes, how the street they are on differs from others in the community, and so on.

Don't try to minimize these differences. They could be worth tens of thousands of dollars when it comes time to sell. Homes on one side of a street, a simple difference, in some neighborhoods sell for $10,000 more than those on the other side.

Most important of all, these differences in homes may be invisible electronically. You may not have a clue when you see pictures or videos or read a description. But drive up and, immediately, it's apparent.

In the next chapter we'll see what specifically to look for when you first see your next home.

4 CHAPTER

WHEN SHOULD I PHYSICALLY CHECK OUT THE PROPERTY?

You had better be happy with the property you buy because, unless you're buying it as an investment, you're going to be living there. That's why you should always check it out physically *before* making the purchase.

Never mind how you can virtually see the property by means of photos, videos, and written descriptions. You're not going to occupy it virtually, but physically, so go there and check it out.

Okay, you'll go there. But, once you get to the property, what should you look for? It's one thing to look at all the facts and figures, it's another to look at the actual bedrooms, baths, and flooring. How do you determine if this is the house for you? How do you determine if it's in good enough shape for you to make an offer? It's not hard and we'll see how in this chapter.

DO YOU LIKE IT?

There are many factors that will determine if you like the property you visit. For the time being, we're going to put aside financial considerations (which will be considered in great detail in the remaining chapters) and concentrate simply on whether this is the right place for you. How do you know?

HINT

Remember, all real estate is unique. No one piece is identical to another. Besides, at some point you're going to have to leave that computer and move to the new property. Better you should see it for the first time before you buy, rather than after.

At the end of this chapter you'll find a list of what usually determines whether a person will like a particular home. You may want to tear or clip out this list and take it with you on your first visit. It will help to clarify what can be an emotional decision.

It's the lucky buyer who gets a distinct, clear impression of a property the first time through. If you love it, you can proceed with the purchase (although I always suggest coming back a second time, just to be sure). If you hate it, you can drop it and look elsewhere.

But, what if you're unsure, as so many of us are? What if there are many points you like, but some you don't like? What do you do then?

Perhaps an analysis of the various parts of the house will help to make a decision easier.

DOES THE NEIGHBORHOOD MAKE A GOOD FIRST IMPRESSION?

The old saying goes that you never get a second chance to make a good first impression. That certainly applies to homes. When you drive to your potential next home through the neighborhood, you'll be all eyes, looking at the neighbors' homes, their yards, the kids (or lack of them) on the street, the neatness (or messiness) of the homes, the nicely painted (or graffiti-painted) fences, and so on.

You'll be forming an overall impression of the neighborhood and, specifically, the block on which your next home will be. That impression can be good—or bad. And there's not much you can do (or should do) to try to influence it. Let your eyes and your mind wander. Absorb what you see and let your brain process it. That first impression is critical. It tells you what you really think about the area of the home.

What produces a good first impression or a bad one? I've identified five neighborhood features. You may want to think about these as you drive up to your home.

Is the Street Itself in Good Shape?

Is it wide with sidewalks on both sides? (In some exclusive areas, there are no sidewalks, but lawns come right down to the street, and this is considered a plus.) Is the pavement in good condition, or is it cracked, broken, and stained? Are the sidewalks in good shape, or are there bulges where tree roots have pushed them up; are there cracks that haven't been fixed? You might not realize it, but the pavement and sidewalks themselves either look nice and neat or rubbishy. How they look will influence what you, and future buyers, think of the neighborhood.

Are the Front Yards of Homes in Good Shape?

Look closely as you approach the home you're interested in. Are all the yards of nearby houses well kept, the lawns mowed, shrubs trimmed, flowers adding color, and with the occasional shade tree? Well-maintained front yards can give a neighborhood a highly desirable, parklike appearance.

On the other hand, have some of the neighbors let their lawns go to weed? Are there garbage cans left out from the last garbage collection day? Are there broken cars being repaired on lawns? These are all signs of a neighborhood in which the owners have little or no pride of ownership, an area in which you might feel uncomfortable and that will make reselling the home later on far more difficult.

HINT

One of the reasons your first impression is so important is that one day when it's time to resell, potential buyers will be doing the same thing. They'll be driving through the neighborhood, and if you like it, chances are they will too, and will stop to see your house. On the other hand, if you have a negative first impression, they may too, and may never even stop by. A home that gives a bad first impression will be much harder to resell.

HINT

Keep in mind that pavement can be changed. The city can come in and repave the street and fix the sidewalks. If they're bad when you buy and the city later does a fix up, it could increase the value of your property!

Is It a Loud and Noisy or Quiet Neighborhood?

Of course, a lot depends on what time of the day and what day of the week you come by. During weekday mornings almost all neighborhoods tend to be quiet. Most people are at work, their children at school. But, what's it like on evenings and weekends? It's worth a trip back to find out.

If you're a retired couple, or empty nesters whose kids have left home, you might not be happy with a neighborhood filled with children playing on sidewalks and even in the street. On the other hand, if you've got kids of your own, you might be sizing up the neighborhood kids as future playmates for your own kids. You might be thrilled to see lots of kids running around.

Also, lots of neighbors on the streets walking around, working on projects, talking or even hollering, lots of dogs barking, and many teenagers suggest that the neighborhood might be noisy, even at night. Do you want this? On the other hand, an area with few people around, even on weekends or evenings, suggests a quieter area.

Is There Any Graffiti?

Graffiti painted on fences or on the walls of homes suggests there may be gang activity in the area. Of course, you probably already checked this out when you looked at the crime statistics. Sometimes, however, you can be surprised. No graffiti of any kind, on the other hand, suggests either there are no gangs, or the neighbors are quick to repaint, or both, probably good signs depending on your persuasion.

Also, look for cyclone fences around front yards, steel bars on windows, and steel doors in the front of homes. All of these suggest that the neighborhood is being impacted by crime of some sort. Even if it's only minor vandalism, is it something you want to deal with? Do you want to live in a neighborhood in which window bars and strong fences are a necessity? It's something you should ask yourself.

Are There Any Detracting Influences?

Finally, is there anything close to the neighborhood that might be a detracting influence?

What's a detracting influence? It could be almost anything. On one end of the spectrum is a toxic dump site. No one would want to live near that.

However, sometimes something as desirable as a shopping center can be detracting, if it's too close. It's nice to be able to walk to shopping. But, what if that shopping is right near where you live, where you can see lights from the parking lot and hear noises from cars coming and going.

Similarly, you want to be near schools. Even if you don't have school-age kids, the person who buys your house later on, when you decide to resell, might have them. And being near a school is a big plus. Unless you're too near.

A friend once bought a home that turned out to back up to a high school football field. She didn't realize it at the time, even though the sellers disclosed it in documents, because the lot was pie shaped in the back and only the very tip touched the back fence of the field. She certainly knew about it, however, on Friday nights when football games were held. Or on other nights when there were events in the stadium and the lights were on and people were cheering. Later on it became difficult for her to sell the property because of this factor.

Be sure you drive around the neighborhood as well as directly through it to the house you're considering. It will only take a few minutes. You might discover that there's a factory nearby, or a transit terminal, or a gas station. Almost anything can crop up in a neighborhood. And, as we've seen, although many things can be desirable at a short distance, they can be most undesirable when too close.

DOES THE HOUSE MAKE A GOOD FIRST IMPRESSION?

It's called "curb appeal." How does the house you're considering look when you first drive up?

Don't underestimate curb appeal. It's one of the strongest determiners of whether you will like or dislike the property. Remember, first impressions are incredibly important.

Some of the factors that go into curb appeal can easily be defined and we'll look at several shortly. Others, however, are vague and undefinable. It may simply be how the house is placed on the lot.

WARNING
Watch out for homes that are cluttered with furniture. Over time, most of us accumulate all sorts of things that we really could do without. Often we add tables, chairs, and knickknacks to our home and expect others to appreciate them as much as we do. If you visit a home for sale and find it cluttered to the point at which you can't imagine how people could live like that, just concentrate on walls, ceilings, and floors. Try to imagine the place without anything in it. I know it's hard, but try to avoid letting other people's furnishings distract you.

I recently was considering a home in a wonderful neighborhood that had poor curb appeal. When I first drove up I was given a bad impression, even though the front yard and lawn were kept up and the home's physical appearance was neat and trim.

What was the problem, I asked myself? I came back a second time approaching from the other side and again felt the home had poor curb appeal. It just looked awkward.

I finally decided that although the neighboring homes were all perpendicular to the street, this home had an irregularly shaped lot and was placed at an angle to the street. One front corner jutted forward giving the appearance that the house had been twisted and placed incorrectly on the lot. That was it, nothing more; however, it was enough to keep me from buying the property. I figured if it bothered me, it would bother many other potential buyers when it came time to resell, meaning it would take me longer and there would be less profit to be had. A good reason to pass.

We've already touched on some of what tends to make a good first impression of a home. Here, again, are those, plus some others:

1. A well-trimmed lawn.
2. Manicured shrubs and hedges.
3. Lots of pretty flowers.
4. A clean driveway (not stained with oil) that isn't cracked. A broken and cracked driveway makes an incredibly bad first impression.
5. A good paint job on the house, including trim (not dull and peeling paint).

6. An overall cheery look that comes from shutters, a welcome mat at the front door, new or polished front door hardware, and so on.

7. A good-looking roof. (It doesn't make much difference what the roof is made of, except that if it has broken tiles, missing shingles, is stained, has upturned tar/fiberglass shingles, it will look bad.) Remember, a large part of what you first see when you look at a house is the roof, and if it looks worn and tired, so will the house.

ARE YOU IMPRESSED BY THE INTERIOR OF THE HOME?

Usually, there are a few things that will immediately make an impression on you, good or bad. Depending on how you react to these, you'll either like or dislike the home.

Is the Carpeting in Good Shape?

What's the condition of the flooring, particularly if it's carpeted? Most of us tend to look down as we walk, and if the carpet is worn and stained, it will make us feel that the home is tired and old. Keep in mind, however, that carpeting and even other kinds of flooring can easily be changed. You may want to factor the cost of doing so into the price.

Is the Paint on the Walls and Ceilings in Good Shape?

Just as with the carpeting, this can make a home look bright and cheery or dull, tired, and old. Many wise sellers will repaint their entire home before putting it on the market. Others simply don't care or don't know and leave old paint, along with stains and marks, as is.

Once again, keep in mind that you can easily and inexpensively repaint a home.

WARNING
You can't easily change the layout of a house. It was literally set in the concrete (the foundation) when it was built. Sometimes clever remodeling can move things around and make them better. But, be sure that's something you're willing to take on when you buy a home with a bad layout.

HINT

Do I have to see the property before I make an offer or afterward? The answer is you can do it either way; however, it makes more sense to see it before you make an offer and purchase. You can, however, stick a clause into the purchase agreement allowing you to back out after you examine the property. This does, however, significantly weaken the offer.

Alternatively, some states allow buyers a period of time (it's three days in California) to back out of a home purchase after they've seen the

You can probably do it yourself in a couple of weekends, so don't let bad paint take the wind out of your sails. But do factor it into the price you offer. You might get a few thousand dollars' discount for the price of a few gallons of paint.

Do You Like the Layout?

This is critical. Yet, very likely, you won't know if you actually like the layout of the home until you experience it. Trying to imagine how it will look from a diagram sent on the Internet or even a video recorded while walking through it can lead to surprising results. Some things may be exactly as you anticipated. Others may come as a complete surprise. You could hate it! Or you could love it more than you thought you would.

Some homes seem to flow naturally from the entrance to the living room to the family room to the kitchen to the bedrooms. The hallways aren't too long, too dark, or too narrow. The kitchen is logically placed as are all the other rooms. It's a layout you can live with.

On the other hand, some layouts are awkward. A friend once asked me about a home he was considering, but which had an awkward layout. When you entered, the first thing you saw were the stairs leading up to the second floor. You had to sort of go around them, then through a tunnel-like hall to get to the kitchen, which was tiny. Next to the kitchen was the family room, which had a fireplace that did not face the open side toward the kitchen, as one would expect it to, but instead was on a sidewall and faced a door that led out to the garage. In short, the layout was horrible and I said so.

My friend said he agreed, but thought that he could stand to live in it because the price was low. I pointed out that the price was probably low because of the bad layout. Furthermore, when it came time for him to resell, he would likewise have to sell for a lower price and have a hard time finding buyers. Better to pay a little more and get a better layout, I suggested.

Does the Kitchen Work for You?

Some kitchens work and some don't. It can be the layout, the countertop, the cabinets, whether the dishwasher is to the left or right of the sink, whether there's a tile floor, linoleum, or wood.

Remember, even if you don't cook a lot, you'll still spend a lot of time in the kitchen. (It's where the refrigerator is!) If you like the kitchen, it might be enough to sway you about the entire house. If you dislike it, then you'll have to consider whether it's bad enough to make you walk away, whether you can live with it, or whether you're prepared to remodel it once you buy. (Keep in mind, probably the most expensive part of a home to remodel is the kitchen.)

The kitchen is one area in which pictures often do justice. You may ask for and receive photos (or images on-line) of the kitchen before you go out to the property. Chances are if you liked it in the picture, you'll love it in real life.

Is the Master Bedroom Liveable?

You'll also spend a lot of time in the master bedroom, albeit sleeping. You'll want to be sure it's big enough for all of your furniture.

seller's disclosures. If your state offers such a backout period and the disclosures aren't given to you until after you make the purchase, you can use this as a way to tie up the property until you see it and then still be able to back out. Just be sure, however, that you see it in a timely fashion!

As I said, however, what makes the most sense is to check it out before making the offer. That way, you run no risks of legal entanglements from an irate seller, and you can make the strongest offer possible.

Does it have an airy window? Is the master bath conveniently located off of it?

I once bought a home with a long, narrow master bedroom. My wife said the shape was horrible, but the house had enough other nice features to make us go forward with the purchase. Then I took a corner of the room and added a built-in fireplace. It changed the entire shape of the room and made it quite comfy and nice. You can remake most master bedrooms, if you're willing to spend the time, effort, and money.

Are the Bathrooms Okay?

You undoubtedly want clean, fresh bathrooms. Look for tile, which is the most desired feature in a bath. Is it in good shape, or cracked and broken? What about the tub, shower, and sink? Will they need to be fixed or replaced? These can be expensive items to work on.

Like a bedroom or kitchen, you can remodel bathrooms. But again, the expense can be high. Are you prepared to spend the money, or can you live with them the way they are?

HOW DO YOU LIKE THE GARAGE AND YARD?

In talking with people who have found their home on-line, the biggest single surprise comes from viewing the yard and the next biggest from viewing the garage. For some reason, pictures, videos, and written descriptions never seem to do justice to either.

Often the yard is bigger and prettier than the buyer thought it would be. Although on a few occasions it can be smaller and in worse shape than anticipated. Is that wonderful lemon tree you saw in a video actually a plum? Have all the roses that were in bloom in the pictures since died from lack of watering? Is the pool full of scale and algae? Are the cement deck and walkways cracked?

On the other hand, is the lot much larger and more beautiful than you imagined? Is the home situated on a little rise from which you get a really marvelous view? Is the lawn rich and thick when you walk on it?

Similarly, although you may have learned that it was a one-, two-, or three-car garage, actually seeing the inside, often crowded with stored materials, can come as a real shock. On the other hand, maybe there's a wonderful workbench in there that comes as a delightful surprise.

The garage and yard can rarely be described electronically in an adequate way. You just have to see them, just as you have to see the neighborhood and the home itself to know whether you want to live there. Going there and actually checking them out, therefore, is a must.

Purchase Decision–Making Factors

1. Overall first impression? Favorable ☐ Unfavorable ☐

2. Neighborhood appearance? Favorable ☐ Unfavorable ☐

3. Home appearance? Favorable ☐ Unfavorable ☐

4. Front yard? Looks good ☐ Looks bad ☐

5. Entrance way? Looks good ☐ Looks bad ☐

6. First impression entering home? Favorable ☐ Unfavorable ☐

7. General layout of rooms? Like it ☐ Hate it ☐

8. Kitchen layout? Favorable ☐ Unfavorable ☐

9. Kitchen appliances, counters, and cabinets? Like them ☐ Hate them ☐

10. Bathrooms? Like them ☐ Hate them ☐

11. Master bedroom? Like it ☐ Hate it ☐

12. Fireplace(s)? Can live with them ☐ Can't stand them ☐

13. Garage big enough? Yes ☐ No ☐

14. Backyard first impression Like it ☐ Hate it ☐

15. Overall impression after seeing property Like it ☐ Hate it ☐ Unsure ☐

5
CHAPTER

WORKING ON-LINE WITH AGENTS AND SELLERS

As soon as you begin earnestly searching for a home on-line, you'll come in contact with agents and For Sale by Owners (FSBOs). Should you work closely with one agent? Should you have many? How much should you tell an agent or a FSBO (pronounced "fizzbo")? In short, how closely or distantly do you want to work with agents and sellers?

The answer is really up to you. Particularly with electronic house hunting, you can get close or keep your distance without hassle. Let's start with agents. (We'll consider FSBOs later in this chapter.)

WHAT'S THE DIFFERENCE BETWEEN DEALING WITH AN AGENT IN PERSON AND ELECTRONICALLY?

When you buy electronically, no agent is going to drag you from home to home in a car until you're exhausted (and perhaps buy something just to be done with it all). No agent is going to be at your elbow encouraging you to make a purchase so they can get a commission. (In real estate, agents don't normally get paid until and unless you buy.)

On the other hand, when you deal with an agent over the phone or e-mail, you're probably going to find that the agent keeps encouraging you to come on down, meet with him or her personally, and see the house. The reason is that an agent who shows you a house personally is usually enti-

47

tled to at least a part of a commission, even if you buy that house from a different agent (within a reasonably short period of time). However, an agent whom you contact only over the Internet about a home cannot normally command a commission if you eventually buy from someone else.

Shopping electronically, in this sense, is like window shopping. You're simply gathering information. You're not locked into an agent in any way until he or she actually takes you to see the property.

WHAT IS YOUR RELATIONSHIP WITH THE AGENT WHEN YOU DEAL ELECTRONICALLY?

Every time you call up a listed house on the Internet, you can be sure it has a listing agent. You are anonymous, however, when you just check out a Web site or a few Web pages describing the house. However, as soon as you contact the agent either by e-mail, phone, or fax and ask for more information, photos, videos, or whatever, you're no longer just another hit on the Web site. You're a prospect, a potential buyer/client.

Although the agent may shower you with information apparently gratis, that agent's real goal is to get you as a client. That agent wants you to be so intrigued by the property that you'll go and see it. He or she wants you to be so impressed with his or her knowledge of the homes in the area and real estate in general that even if the house in question turns out not to be what you want, you'll let him or her show you other property . . . and will eventually buy from him or her. That, after all, is how agents make their living.

However, as indicated earlier, you are under no obligation. You don't have to run out and meet the agent; you can simply get the information. And then, if you're not interested, pass on the property . . . and the agent. On the other hand, if you are indeed impressed with the person, you may want to establish a business relationship with them.

HOW MUCH SHOULD YOU TELL THE AGENT (OR SELLER)?

Beyond the obvious fact that you're looking for a home, you're not really obligated to pass along any other information. However, agents and sellers will naturally want to know more. There are two reasons. The first is that they will want to know if you are a serious buyer. In other words, do you have the cash for the down payment and closing costs? And do you have the wherewithal to get financing? If you don't, they're wasting their time with you.

Second, agents (not sellers) will want to "qualify" you so that if you can't purchase the home you're initially contacting them about, perhaps they can find another home that will suit your needs and ability to purchase. This now raises the issue of whether you actually want to work with the agent in question, which we deal with elsewhere in this chapter.

My advice is that if you are, indeed, interested in the property, or the agent, you do pass along enough information to keep them mollified. Indicate that you have enough cash to make the deal (don't be too specific—you don't want to give up a negotiating position), and that you can handle the payments.

SHOULD I PICK AN AGENT BY AREA?

It's important to remember that all agents are local. They only know their local area. It would be a waste of your time and unethical conduct on their part for an agent to attempt to show you property outside of his or her region. For example, although an agent may know the San Fernando Valley of Los Angeles, he or she may be totally unfamiliar with the South Bay area, only twenty-five miles away. You need to pick an agent who knows a local area.

For example, you've decided on one particular area, say the Scottsdale area near Phoenix, Arizona. If you know of a knowledgeable, courteous, reliable, effective agent with whom you are comfortable, you would be wise to use that person exclusively to look at properties in Scottsdale.

On the other hand, let's say that you picked out two areas you were considering.

HINT

A good way to demonstrate that you can afford to buy the property is to get pre-approved by a lender and have a lender's letter to show. It will indicate that the lender is committed to loan you up to a certain amount on the purchase of a qualifying home. If you want, you can get a separate letter for each property you are interested in, and the amount can be the minimum loan needed. (You don't want to tip your hand by showing you can qualify for a higher loan—this could hurt you on the negotiations.)

HINT

In theory, any agent can sell you any property. That includes properties listed on the Internet. Agent Dorothy, who has the property on Maple Street listed electronically, can sell you Agent Sam's house electronically listed on Sycamore Street. There are some exceptions. Occasionally, an agent has a property that he or she feels is so easy to sell that they will refuse to cobroke it, to work with other agents. This is unusual, however, because most sellers won't hear of it.

Scottsdale was one. But Tucson, a couple of hours away, was another. Now, you would be wise to use two agents, one for each region. You wouldn't expect the Scottsdale agent to be able to service you adequately in Tucson and vice versa.

WHAT ABOUT THE AGENT WHO HAS LISTED THE HOME I'M INTERESTED IN ON THE INTERNET?

But, you may argue, what about all the agents who have homes listed on the Internet? You've picked out seven homes and, as a result, you've made contact with seven agents. Shouldn't you respect them and go with a separate agent to each property?

I wouldn't, unless I didn't really have one agent I liked. Find an agent you like in the area you're considering and work with him or her.

As you contact agents about different properties, you will undoubtedly write to them via e-mail as well as talk to them over the phone. One may stand out as the person you want to deal with. Until you discover otherwise, this is the person for you.

HOW DO I FIND A REALLY GOOD AGENT?

The rules here are the same, whether it's in person or electronically (except that for your purposes, you undoubtedly will want an agent who is Internet literate). Here's how you qualify a real estate agent to determine if you want to work with them.

How Active Are They?

Ask them how many properties they've listed in the last six months. Also, ask how many buyers they've represented in sales over the past six months.

These are two separate questions. You want to work with someone who is actively in the business, someone who sells, on average, a house or more per month.

Furthermore, you don't want to work just with a "lister"; some agents only list property and rely on others to make the sale. This agent may be at a disadvantage when the time comes for serious negotiations, both being out of practice and, perhaps, not being very good at it.

Whom Does the Agent Represent?

Ask the agent if they will represent you. In real estate the agent owes a fiduciary responsibility to either the seller *or* the buyer or (in some strange cases) both. If you're dealing with the agent who listed the property, that person is either the seller's agent or agrees to try to represent both the seller and you, the buyer (not a good arrangement, as we'll see).

On the other hand, once you find an agent you like, you can ask him or her if they will represent you exclusively, become a buyer's agent. Any agent can do this, and in some parts of the country, buyers' agents are rapidly becoming a major force in real estate.

Who Recommends the Agent?

Ask the agent for references. They should be able to supply you with the names, addresses, and phone numbers of at least three clients they have successfully worked with over the past six months. Call these

HINT

Just because an agent has listed a property on the Internet doesn't mean that you are any more obligated to deal directly with that person than you would be if an agent listed a home that you saw in the newspaper. You could contact the agent and ask for more basic information. But, you could also explain you were working with someone else and when it came time to see the property, that other agent would show it to you. Remember, the listing agent gets a piece of the commission no matter who sells the property, so he or she should be more than willing to help you in any way possible.

WARNING

Some agents are part-timers. They only work a few hours a week. This person usually doesn't have enough invested in the business to really know the market or to serve you properly. You want a full-time agent, someone who makes a living selling real estate.

people up. See what they have to say about the agent. You could be quite surprised, for good . . . or for bad.

How Long in the Business?

Ask the agent how long he or she has been in the business. It usually takes at least five years to learn the housing market in an area and how to really handle real estate negotiations. You want someone experienced who can get the job done right for you. You don't want someone to be learning on your watch.

Big Office or Little?

Don't pay too much attention to whether the agent has a big or a little office. Selling real estate is a personal business. You want to deal with a good person. It really doesn't matter if that person is the only one in the office or is a member of a billion-dollar national chain. It's the personal service that counts.

Large chains, however, do offer certain advantages. For example, when you go into a McDonald's or Burger King anywhere in the country (or the world for that matter) you know you're going to get at least the minimum standard of quality that the company stands for. The burger may not be filet mignon, but it won't be leather either.

Many large, as well as small, offices have their own Web sites these days. (When you check, be sure you're clear about whether you're at the national office or a local broker's site.) National franchises offer central Web sites such as:

www.century21.com
www.coldwellbanker.com
www.remax.com
www.era.com

WHEN SHOULD I SWITCH AGENTS?

Any time an agent isn't servicing you, dump him or her. Remember, they are getting paid well for the job, and the job they are supposed to be performing is servicing your real estate needs. If they're not doing the job adequately, find someone else who will.

There are two big complaints that buyers usually have about agents. The first is that the agent doesn't pay enough attention to them. The agent shows them a few houses and if they don't buy, that agent hands them a card, says to keep in touch, and is gone.

When you buy on-line, that usually isn't a problem. You're not really counting on the agent to find properties for you to see. You've already found them. You're counting on the agent only to show you the property and, presumably, to handle the paperwork and the negotiations.

The second problem is that buyers complain that the agent isn't compatible with them. This usually translates into the fact that the agent is too pushy, acting too assertively in trying them get them to purchase. Or the agent does something that the buyers don't feel is proper. (He or she says something about a house that later proves to be untrue or tries to pressure them in some way that they later realize was unfair or, perhaps, unethical or even illegal.)

Whatever the reason, if it turns out that you don't get along with your agent, don't wait, don't argue, don't threaten. Just dump the agent and get another. There are plenty of excellent agents out there, and a whole bunch of them are waiting in line to get your business.

HINT

The agent represents whomever he or she declares they are representing. It doesn't matter who pays the commission. Very often a seller will end up paying the buyer's agent's commission as part of the usual split that agents are familiar with.

SHOULD I REPORT AN AGENT WHOSE ACTIVITIES I CONSIDER UNETHICAL OR ILLEGAL?

Again, that depends. Unless you're quite familiar with real estate ethics and law, how do you know that what the agent said or did is really wrong?

WARNING
An agent can declare that he or she is representing both the buyer and seller— a "dual" agent. This means that the agent, presumably, is on both your sides. However, just as a slave can only serve one master, an agent can truly only serve one client. For example, if you tell the agent that you'll offer $200,000, but that you're really willing to pay $210,000, does the dual agent tell the seller? A seller's agent is obligated to tell the seller. A buyer's agent is obligated not to speak! What does the dual agent do? Duality in agency is a legal concept that makes little sense in the real world.

Maybe they were acting appropriately and you just didn't understand. Furthermore, listing and selling on the Internet is a brand new area, and only now are accepted rules and standards for ethical conduct being defined. Perhaps what you're upset about is a completely new area not only for you, but for real estate agents in general, and everyone is just feeling their way.

If you're really upset, contact the agent's local real estate board. (They probably have a Web site and you can do it electronically!) Although this is a trade organization run by and for agents, these boards usually don't want to see any hanky panky that could result in a bad name for their membership, and if something really bad did happen, they may be more than willing to help you.

In addition, you can also contact the state licensing department for real estate. They also can be helpful. However, be sure you're clear on why you're doing this. Do you want to get even? Did you lose money and want to get it back (in which case a lawyer may be your best bet)? Or do you want to see that someone else doesn't run into the same problems you did? Sometimes, particularly if there was no real damage done, it's easier to just get on with your life and house hunt and let bygones be bygones.

SHOULD I CONTACT FSBO (FOR SALE BY OWNER) SELLERS DIRECTLY?

Certainly. They are waiting for your call. At any given time, as many as 15 to 20 percent of the homes for sale in the country are offered directly by sellers with no real estate agent. If you ignore this large share of the market, you could miss just the one house that's perfect for you.

FSBOs tend to list on the Internet. The reason is simple: they want the exposure. Whereas agents have a huge network of cobroking agents to work with, not to mention the advertising power and name recognition of major brokerage offices, FSBOs have only themselves. They have to pay for expensive advertising for the one property they have to sell. If you don't like it, they can't try to sell you something else.

In short, for a FSBO, getting buyers to find their home has always been the big stumbling block, until the Internet came along. Now, a FSBO can put up a listing, and it can be found just as easily as an agent's property. For a relatively small cost, probably a couple of hundred dollars, FSBOs get big publicity.

CAN I GET A BETTER DEAL WITH A FSBO?

Sometimes. Because the FSBO is not paying a commission, he or she may lower the price of the house by all or a portion of the amount that would otherwise have gone to an agent. That could amount to a discount of 5 or 6 percent or more. (Agents' commissions are completely negotiable.) On a $200,000 home, that could amount to an immediate discount of $10,000 to $12,000—nothing to sneeze at.

Furthermore, as noted earlier, the FSBO may be just the house you want, whereas those homes which are listed may not fill the bill for you. In other words, a FSBO gives you an additional source of homes to search.

IS THERE A BIG ADVANTAGE TO DEALING WITH A FSBO ELECTRONICALLY?

Perhaps the biggest advantage that the Internet gives to you and to FSBOs is the ability to inquire and later conduct negotiations electronically (also see the next chapter) at a distance. Quite frankly, it's very hard to deal with the seller face-to-face. Indeed, one of the biggest services an agent performs is to be a go-between for the buyer and the seller. You can run down the property to the agent; the seller can run you down to the agent. But the agent, acting as a buffer, keeps animosities out of the negotiations and thus helps smooth the way to a successful deal.

HINT

Don't be confused by real estate terminology. It's really quite simple and it's the same in every state. An *agent* is the generic term for anyone who is licensed to sell real estate. A *broker* is an agent who can work for himself or herself; can open an office; can, so to speak, hang out a shingle. A *salesperson* is an agent who does not have enough experience to work for him- or herself, but instead must work under the tutelage of a broker. (Sometimes, for financial reasons, a broker will accept

The same thing can happen when dealing with a seller electronically. You can be perfectly respectful with what you write by e-mail, all the while swearing under your breath at the seller, who may be doing the same at you.

Unfortunately, this sometimes goes the other way. It's easy to allow rage to rule your comments when dealing with something as impersonal as e-mail, and you can say things you'll later regret. However, it's also much easier to overlook negative comments from the other party.

I've dealt with sellers via e-mail who were vehement in their comments at first. But, once we got to know each other electronically, they settled down and an amicable relationship developed.

In general, I've found that electronic conversations with sellers tend to be a great and beneficial buffer.

IS IT EASY TO WORK WITH A FSBO?

It doesn't have to be hard. But, it can often be more difficult than working with an agent. Here are some of the problems you may face.

FSBOs May Have an Unrealistic Price

One of the reasons a person may try to sell FSBO is because he or she doesn't like the realistic price that agents have quoted for the property. This person thinks their house is worth much more than comparable homes and feels they can get their price themselves. Thus, you may have difficulty getting them to negotiate down.

FSBOs Often List with Themselves to Save the Commission, So They May Not Offer a Bargain to You

Because the FSBO isn't paying a commission, as noted they are saving upward of 6 percent on the sales price (whatever they would pay on a commission) when compared with a listed property. You would think they would pass along some or all of the savings to the buyer to get a quicker sale. But, many FSBOs are adamant; they won't split or give up part or all of the commission. They want it all to themselves. Hence, whereas you as a buyer may anticipate getting a bargain price, you may find that you actually pay no less (sometimes more) with a FSBO.

FSBOs May or May Not Be Aware of Disclosure Laws That Apply to Them

Real estate agents, presumably, are aware of all of the pitfalls involved in a real estate transaction, particularly the disclosure requirements of most states. FSBOs may not be aware of these and other seller requirements. Thus, they may not be willing to disclose defects or easily allow you to have an inspection of the property. In short, they may simply be ignorant of what's required of them, making your job of purchasing all the more difficult.

FSBOs May Not Understand the Paperwork

A real estate transaction involves a sales contract, an escrow that may require the

the status of a salesperson and work as a salesperson under the license of another broker.) A *Realtor* © is a broker who is a member of the National Association of Realtors (NAR), a trade organization. It has almost a million members nationwide, and there are affiliate organizations in every state and in almost every city. A *Realtor Associate* is a salesperson who works for a Realtor/broker and is also a member of the NAR. Got it? If not, just think of the Realtor/broker as the top dog in the real estate pyramid.

HINT

If buyer and seller are agreeable to the basics, such as purchase price and financing, it should be possible to get an attorney or an agent to handle the actual transaction for a set fee. Attorneys who specialize in real estate will typically do this for under $1000.

seller to clear the title, and other documentation as needed. But the FSBO may have done no more planning than to think he or she can sell the property "with a handshake." You may have to educate the FSBO as to what's really needed, a daunting task.

FSBOs May Not Tolerate Any Criticism of the Property

You may discover that the roof leaks, that the furnace is broken, that there's a crack in the foundation, or that there are any number of other problems with the home. You want it all fixed or you want a discount on the price to compensate. But, the FSBO simply won't hear of any problems with their beloved home. Because it's theirs, it has to be perfect. Hence, you may find that it's very hard to conduct reasonable negotiations with a FSBO.

In short, when you're dealing with a real estate professional, you can expect to be treated professionally. When you're dealing with a FSBO, however, you can expect to be dealt with by an amateur.

WHAT CAN I DO TO HELP MAKE THE DEAL WITH A FSBO?

If you're well versed in real estate transactions, you can guide the FSBO. Once your credentials are established, many FSBOs will go along, as long as whatever you propose seems reasonable and fair.

Or, you can get the aid of a professional: an agent or an attorney. It may be worth the cost (which the seller probably should pay) to have someone who knows the ropes to handle the actual transaction. When a buyer and seller have already found each other, agents will often be willing to conclude the transaction for a smaller commission, no more than half the regular fee and sometimes much less.

HOW SHOULD I APPROACH AN ON-LINE FSBO?

Do it the same way you would with an agent. Contact them by e-mail or go to their Web site. (Yes, many FSBOs will construct their own Web site just to facilitate the sale of their home!)

Talk to them over the phone, gathering as much information as you would with a listed property. Get the details. This also helps you to establish repartee, a bond of trust that will help oil the transaction.

Go to the property. Physically inspect it. Look it over. Determine if it's what you want.

If it's something you like, work out how you'll handle the paperwork. Get an attorney or agent to help, if you're not experienced in real estate yourself.

Arrange the financing. Don't expect any help from the FSBO here. You're on your own. But, as we'll see in Chapter 6, financing real estate on the Internet is becoming increasingly easy, and can save you money.

6

CHAPTER

MAKING THE ON-LINE OFFER

Once you've found a house that you like, have checked it out (Chapter 4), and now want to purchase it, the next step is to make an offer on it. You propose to buy it at a certain price and with specific terms. If the sellers accept, you're on your way to ownership.

Historically this has always been done on paper. Indeed, from a legal point of view, a contract to purchase real estate is not enforceable unless it is in writing. However, this has always been compared with an oral offer in which, for example, you simply say you're willing to buy a piece of property. You can't be held to your oral declaration.

The question now arises of the possibility of making an on-line offer. It's in writing, isn't it? Can you do it? Is it enforceable?

Like much of what's happening with electronic communications, we're into a gray area that really has no precedent and in which the rules are being established as we go. If you write out an offer to purchase and electronically send it to someone who accepts, is it legally binding?

Perhaps a comparison with an earlier form of electronic communications would be helpful. It wasn't that many years ago that faxes were new. Virtually anything written can be faxed, yet at first in real estate transactions, faxed contracts to purchase were simply not accepted.

Today, however, particularly when the parties are some distance apart,

61

H I N T

Remember that a fax can be transmitted and received entirely by a computer. In what way, therefore, is it different from e-mail?

faxed contracts are commonplace. Indeed, I've purchased many properties by means of fax. I send (or receive) an offer by fax. I make changes, sign, and fax back. And so it goes, back and forth, until there's agreement. Finally we end up with a faxed copy on which everyone has signed signatures.

Will a fax hold up?

Maybe. I do know that I always insist on the actual written document to be sent and countersigned subsequent to the faxes. The faxes are done because of speed. But, they are always followed by the actual signed written agreement.

Of course, e-mail is different. There is no signature. And there always remains the possibility of changing something that's transmitted. It's only the stroke of a keyboard to change an e-mail message.

Yet, I regularly buy airline tickets and other products through e-mail without a signature using only a credit card number. I can even electronically transfer funds of any amount from bank to bank. Why not real estate?

IS REAL ESTATE DIFFERENT?

In truth, there should be no difference. And yet there is. At the present time, as a buyer, I would not feel confident in relying on an offer that was forwarded to me electronically. There's too much opportunity for the other party to say, "That's not exactly what I sent," or, "It wasn't me that sent it."

This is not to say that there aren't methods for verifying what was transmitted—there are—or that there aren't ways to determine who was sending the message (social security number, mother's maiden name, or other identifying methods). It's just that I don't feel comfortable with any of these. When I send or receive an offer that I want to be legally binding involving real estate, I want it done the old-fashioned way—in writing. And for the present, I suggest you do, too.

Of course, that's only for the present. We who are involved in electronic communications correctly foresee that in the future the means for legally binding electronic contractual agreements involving real estate will become a reality. When they do, I can assure you I'll take full advantage of them.

DOES THAT MEAN YOU SHOULDN'T MAKE AN ON-LINE OFFER?

Not at all—you can, and probably should, make on-line offers. They're easier to make, quicker, and can clinch a deal for you. Just understand that they may have no more weight than an oral offer—they may not be legally binding. Always follow them up immediately by a signed, written document.

In other words, you may indeed be able to handle some of the negotiations electronically. But when it comes time to be safe, I get it on paper.

A friend of mine recently conducted an on-line negotiation for the purchase of her home. She and the sellers (without benefit of an agent) were both on-line, and after she made the initial offer, she waited for a time until the sellers thought it over and countered on-line.

It went back and forth for nearly four hours and until all the details had been hammered out. Once they were and both she and the sellers agreed, she printed out the terms they had agreed to, took them to her attorney (who drew up a formal sales agreement) and FedExed it to the sellers, who signed and returned copies. The deal was done.

DO I NEED AN ATTORNEY TO FORMALIZE THE OFFER?

It's a good idea. If you're not very familiar with real estate transactions, have an attorney, or at least an agent, prepare the formal sales agreement for you. Remember, it's a legally binding agreement and needs to be done right.

WARNING

Time is always an element in negotiations. You and the seller may agree via electronic mail upon a certain price and terms. But, by the time the actual written offer arrives and needs to be signed, one or the other of you may have changed your mind. Therefore, I suggest that you use faxes as well. Yes, you may want to do your initial negotiating through e-mail, but as soon as you've knocked down what you agree upon, send out a fax and get a signed fax back. And then immediately follow up with a written and signed original written document.

WARNING

As I've said many times, when I first began in real estate more than thirty years ago, the sales agreement was only a single page and most of that was handwritten by the parties involved. Today, most sales agreements are lengthy documents, anywhere from six to ten pages in length filled with legalese. Almost nothing is handwritten with the exception of the price and the loan amount. Everything else, even most contingencies, has language created by

HOW MUCH SHOULD I OFFER?

Having disposed of the means of transmitting offers, let's get down to the nuts and bolts of the offer itself. How much should you offer?

This is, of course, the big question. Offer too much and the sellers will quickly accept, and you'll forever feel you were taken. Offer too little and the sellers may simply not respond, and you could lose out on the house of your dreams. What is the perfect offer?

To begin, it's important to get a good sense of the market. Fortunately, because you're Internet savvy, this should be relatively easy.

The tried-and-true method of determining value in real estate is to check the *comparables*. This refers to recent sales of similar properties. If a home just like the one you're considering sold a month ago for $200,000, then there's an excellent chance that the home you're interested in will go for a similar price, perhaps a bit more or less depending on the direction of the market and the actual differences between the properties.

So how do you find comparables? If you're working with an agent, it should be a piece of cake. Just ask the agent (if she or he doesn't first volunteer) to *electronically* send you a list of the comparables. These are readily available from real estate boards, which almost universally have them recorded electronically. Typically, this list will include all sales in the area within your price range within the past six months to a year.

If you're not working with an agent, you can get the information directly. DataQuick provides information based on assessed value of homes. For $9.95, they'll send you a list of comparable sales within a half mile or so of the property. Up to thirty comparables are available over the past year. Home Shark charges $14.95 for six reports.

www.dataquick.com/consumer/htm

www.homeshark.com

Once you get the list, look at the size of the homes. The stats should give square footage. If it's a tract home, try to find models identical to yours. Typically, this is easiest to do by square footage. For example, there may be three models to the tract:

attorneys designed to withstand a legal challenge. Keep this in mind when you consider handling a transaction with nothing more than a few paragraphs created on e-mail. You want more, much more.

1872 square feet

2169 square feet

2420 square feet

If the home you're considering happens to be 2169 square feet (the agent or seller should be able to provide you with the size), it wouldn't do to compare it with the larger 2420-square-foot model or the smaller 1872-square-foot model. The first will have a much higher price, the second much lower, neither of which will be true comparables for your home. You want to compare sales with other 2169-square-foot homes.

Next, weed it out. Eliminate homes that are significantly different. For example, some homes may have swimming pools and yours doesn't. It's not a comparable, unless you allow a certain amount less for your place because it doesn't have the pool.

Finally, you'll arrive at a group of perhaps two or three homes that are very similar to yours. Now, check out the prices, both listing and sales if available. The list price is

H I N T

Remember, no two homes are exactly alike nor exactly located in the same way. All real estate is unique.

HINT

It is now possible to get an unofficial on-line appraisal. eloan.com offers such appraisals for $14.95. It actually works in most major metropolitan areas (covering about 70 percent of the population). It's important to understand, however, that this on-line estimator of value is not a formal appraisal for a mortgage; it is simply an estimate to help in determining how much to offer.

what the property originally listed for. The sales price is what it finally sold for. In between is how much of a discount the seller accepted.

You may find that homes in your area are typically selling for a discounted price of 5 percent. Or the discount may be more—or less. In a hot market you may find that the homes are selling for *more* than the listed price! In any event, this gives you a clue as to how much less (or more) than the asking price you might want to offer.

From the comparables, you should get a fairly good idea of what the home you're interested in should sell for. But don't overlook the element of time. If the market is going up, say 6 percent per year, and it's been three months since the last sale, you might want to consider adding 1.5-percent (one-fourth of six) to the last sales price to come up with the current price. Adjust the price to market trends to give you a more realistic sense of what the house is worth.

Now, you've got a true sense of value of the home you're interested in. You also can see how realistic is the price the seller is asking. And you should have some sense of how much less than the asking price the typical discount may be.

WHAT IF THERE AREN'T ANY COMPARABLES?

There are always other sales to compare with the home you're considering. The only real question is how similar are the other properties to yours. If you have to go to another tract or area to find sales, the comparables may be way off. In that case, it's more a case of guestimating. Some buyers in such a situation hire an appraiser to come in and give an evaluation of the property. The appraiser, however, is faced with the same dilemma as you—the difficulty in finding comparables. Ultimately, you may simply have to rely on your own best judgement.

SHOULD I LOWBALL THE SELLER?

Let's say that you know, from checking the comparables, that the home is probably worth $200,000. But, does the seller know it? Or is the seller so desperate to sell that he or she will accept any lowball offer? Should you maybe offer $150,000 and take a chance on "stealing" the home?

I have no problem with lowball offers, as long as you're realistic about it. Being realistic means understanding up front that it's a long shot and the seller probably won't accept, or may counteroffer at or close to the list price. Furthermore, while you're playing games lowballing, another buyer could come in with a better offer and buy the property out from under you. (This is particularly a problem in a hot market.)

I understand the risks. And, except in a very hot market, always offer low going in. My offer may not be way low, but it's usually lower than I think the seller will accept. After all, who really knows another person's motivation? Maybe I'll catch the seller when he or she is totally disgusted with the property and the sales process and is ready to take the first stupid offer that comes through the door. If it's mine, I could get a steal.

HOW LONG WILL THE NEGOTIATIONS LAST?

In most transactions involving buying a home, there will be some negotiations. You'll offer one price, the seller will come back with another, and offers will go back

HINT
Your seller may be asking too high a price, or actually too low. By checking the comparables, you'll know and you can adjust your offer accordingly.

WARNING
A seller is under no obligation to deal with only one buyer at a time. Sellers accept offers as they are made, even if a second one comes in while negotiations on a first offer are still in play.

HINT

A savvy seller always counters, but you can't always count on getting a savvy seller. Your seller may simply blow off your low offer and do nothing. Then what do you do? Making another, higher offer after the seller hasn't countered may make you look foolish. But, if it's the house you want, better foolish than not to get the deal.

WARNING

Keep in mind that the money you put up as a deposit is at risk. The less you put up, the less you have at risk.

and forth until there is an agreement of the minds—or not. It won't always happen, but be prepared for lengthy negotiations.

On the other hand, I've talked with buyers who dealt directly with FSBO sellers, both of whom became good friends and who amicably worked out price and terms without lengthy negotiations.

Every deal is different and the only constant is that you never know in advance how it's all going to work out—or if it will.

HOW BIG A DEPOSIT SHOULD I OFFER?

The deposit is money that you put up at the time you make an offer to show that you are in earnest about making the purchase. (You're putting your money where your mouth is, so to speak.) Hence the deposit is actually "earnest money." It demonstrates to the seller that your offer isn't capricious. From a seller's perspective, if you say you'll buy a property, it's one thing. If you say you'll buy it and put up $10,000 cash, that's something else.

An offer can be made without a deposit. However, a seller is less likely to accept it. After all, you have very little to lose by not following through on the deal, unless you put up some cash.

Agents tend to want you to put up a bigger deposit. They argue that this will convince the seller that you are in earnest about buying the property and that it will help make the deal. Not necessarily.

Your deposit can be for any amount. And it's to your advantage to offer as little in a deposit as possible (so you don't tie up your money), with one exception. That exception is when you have a rather poor offer, but want to demonstrate to the seller that you are sincere. A seller faced with a poor offer, might at least consider it, if the deposit is big.

Generally speaking, a deposit of $3000 should be sufficient on properties valued up to about $125,000, $5000 for properties up to $250,000, and $10,000 for more expensive properties. Of course, if the price gets over half a million, then the deposit will need to go up proportionately.

WHAT HAPPENS TO THE DEPOSIT?

It should become part of the down payment. Be sure that your contract, in fact, specifies that it will be handled that way; else, it might be interpreted as money in addition to the down payment!

The only real problem usually occurs when you offer a deposit, the seller accepts the deal, and then, for whatever reason, the deal doesn't go through. You may or may not be entitled to get your deposit back, depending on the circumstances. Generally speaking, if the deal falls through and it's no fault of yours, the deposit is refunded. On the other hand, if you simply change your mind and back out, you could lose it.

HINT

A good attorney or agent will include *contingencies,* in the contract, clauses that will allow you to back out gracefully in certain circumstances and get your deposit back. For example, a standard contingency lets you back out and get your deposit back if you can't get the financing you want and need.

WHAT ABOUT THE DOWN PAYMENT AND THE MORTGAGE?

These will vary depending on your financial condition. You may want to put a lot of money down, if you have it available, to get lower payments. Or, you may want to put a minimum down (10 percent or less) if you have good credit and a strong income and get a bigger mortgage. This maxi-

WARNING

Although the sellers are entitled to the deposit, it's unwise to give it to them directly. They might spend it and not have it available to give back if the deal falls through. A better option is to give it to the agent or to a title insurance/escrow company to hold in trust for the seller.

mizes your investment potential and gives you a bigger tax deduction (taxes and interest, up to certain high limits, are deductible from federal income taxes).

A word about investment potential. If you put $50,000 down on a $200,000 property and later resell for a $10,000 profit, you've made 20 percent on your investment. If, however, you only put $10,000 on the same property and resell for a $10,000 profit, you've made 100 percent on your investment.

Real estate offers the opportunity for high-leverage deals. The lower the down payment, the greater the potential for profit. Keep in mind, however, that the lower the down payment, the higher the mortgage, the corresponding monthly payments, and the risk.

———

However you handle the deal, do it cautiously. You may also want to check into my book, *Tips and Traps When Buying a Home* (McGraw-Hill, 1997), for additional information.

7

CHAPTER

CAN I GET A MORTGAGE ON-LINE?

Although currently still in its infancy, obtaining a mortgage on-line is today the fastest-growing area of real estate finance. In 1998 it did an amazing $10 billion dollars on-line; total mortgage financing for the year, however, was around $1 trillion. Although at present only a select few are using this method, in the future it will probably be the method of choice. The reason is that obtaining your mortgage on-line offers the following advantages:

- Discounts (not available otherwise)
- Privacy
- Speed
- Wide selection of mortgage types
- Competitive interest rates
- Easy tracking of the loan in progress

In this chapter, we'll go through the process of obtaining a mortgage on-line, looking out for the pitfalls as well as pointing out the advantages. However, keep in mind that real estate finance is not a simple subject. If you're not fully up to speed on the types of products offered or the terminology, you might want to occasionally check ahead into the next chapter in which you'll find a mortgage primer.

WARNING

One of the drawbacks of applying for a mortgage on-line is that you pretty much have to know what you want. Although many of the mortgage Web sites provide some information, unless you're familiar with real estate finance, it can all seem very confusing, at least at first. Hopefully, this and Chapter 8 will dispel much of that confusion.

WHERE DO I FIND MORTGAGE WEB SITES?

It's almost the case that if you've been looking for home-listing Web sites, the mortgage sites will find you. They are linked to the listing sites and are often only a key push away. To help locate some of the better sites, I've listed several of those that I've found to be most helpful. Keep in mind, however, that there are literally thousands available.

www.eloan.com

This is one of the best sites currently on the Web. It's pages are clean and it's easy to maneuver around on them. It has virtually any type of current mortgage information you could want. In addition, it also includes a list of actual charges for different mortgages (which almost all lenders include), which you won't find on many other sites. In addition, it goes further than most to try to help you analyze what type of mortgage would be best for your situation by using a series of wizards that lead you through the information you need. This is an excellent place to start (and perhaps to end) your mortgage search.

http://www.chase.com

This is the Web site of Chase Manhattan bank, one of the country's leading banking lenders. You will find virtually all of the mortgage products the bank offers. Some of these may be very suited to your needs, and you may not be able to locate them elsewhere.

http://www.countrywide.com

Countrywide is the largest independent mortgage banking lender in the nation. They have a large Web presence, but when I spoke with a representative, he said that at the time their on-line applications amounted to less than 1 percent of their total loan applications. Their Web site contains a great deal of information, but as of this writing was not kept as up-to-date as others I visited.

http://www.homeshark.com

An independent lender that has an excellent Web site and offers many different loan programs, some with discounts.

http://www.homefair.com

Home Fair is an independent mortgage lender site. Again, they offer a wide variety of mortgage financing.

http://www.namc.com

North American Mortgage is a large mortgage banker that offers a broad range of mortgages. You may find a specific type of mortgage here that you can't find elsewhere.

http://www.mortgage.quicken.com

QuickenMortgage comes from Intuit, the people who have the excellent Quicken home financial programs. I found their wizard/calculator to be one of the best I tried. As of this writing, their site offers mortgages from six national lenders.

http://www.hud.com

The Federal Government Department of Housing and Urban Development (HUD) does not offer mortgages on-line, but it has an incredible wealth of mortgage hunting information that should prove invaluable.

http://www.fanniemae.com

Fannie Mae is the country's largest secondary lender. You won't find many consumer mortgage loans here, but you will find all sorts of information on mortgages. (Much of it, unfortunately, tends to be highly technical.) This is a good resource for the more advanced mortgage hunter.

http://www.freddiemac.com

Freddie Mac is the second largest secondary lender. Again, no loans directly to consumers, but filled with lots of useful information. It tends to be less technical and more consumer oriented than Fannie Mae.

SHOULD I USE THE CALCULATOR AT MORTGAGE SITES?

Many of the tools that you will find on Web sites can help you with your mortgage search. For example, at many mortgage sites you will find a calculator designed to help you determine how big a mortgage you can get. You simply input the amount of the loan and the down payment (the calculator usually knows the current interest rate), and it can give you your mortgage payment (see Figure 7.1).

PLAY "WHAT IF?"

Perhaps one of the biggest benefits of these calculators is that they allow you to try out a variety of different scenarios. For example, you can ask the question, "How will my payment differ if I put more down?" You can input 10 percent down, 20 percent, or even 25 percent, and see how the payment changes.

Or, you can change the loan amount. "What if I borrow $150,000 instead of $140,000? How much will my payments go up?"

In some cases you can change the interest rate. You can ask, "What if the interest goes up 1 percent? Or down? How will it affect my mortgage payments?"

Playing "what if" with the calculator can help you come up with the optimum loan for you.

WHAT ABOUT THE MORTGAGE WIZARDS?

In addition to simple mortgage calculators, some sites also contain mortgage wizards. You are asked to input a few bits of information, such as the

FIGURE 7.1

Mortgage payment calculator.

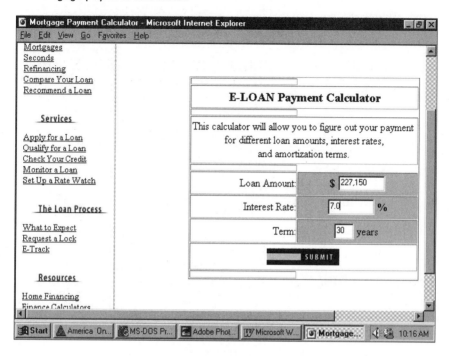

amount of your income, how long you plan to keep the house, how many points you're willing to pay, whether you can handle a mortgage payment that fluctuates, and so on. After entering the information, the wizard recommends the best mortgage type for you. In short, it not only shows you what you can get, but presumably what you want.

Be careful when using wizards. I make it a point to try out the wizards at each mortgage Web site I visit, and although some work very well, I've found many that simply don't tell the real truth. Often they don't ask for enough information to make a realistic recommendation. Other times they are slanted toward one type of mortgage or another. It's one thing for a calculator to determine your monthly payment when you input the mortgage amount, term, and interest rate. That's the simplest of calculations and given the formula, you can do it yourself.

However, it's another thing to recommend a specific type of mortgage financing. It's when a wizard attempts to tell you what you person-

WARNING
Beware of a mortgage site selling the information you give it to others. Each site should offer an explanation of its privacy policy, which should be that the info you submit will never be sent anywhere, other than to complete the mortgage process for you.

ally will be able to get that they can fall down. In short, beware of mortgage wizards. Most of them are not nearly as smart as they claim to be.

WHAT SHOULD I BE AWARE OF WHEN SEARCHING FOR SITES?

The biggest problem with hunting for mortgages on-line is that every mortgage broker in the country (and there are many thousands) seems to have his or her own Web site. Joe Smith in your town may be licensed to handle mortgages. He can throw up a Web site and for very little money, make it seem like the biggest, most important Web presence you've ever seen.

However, Mr. Smith may not have access to many lenders, his fees may be higher than most, and he may not be able to effectively lock you into a mortgage. In addition, he may be limited to issuing mortgages in his hometown area. For example, if Mr. Smith is from Pittsburgh, he may not be able to offer mortgages in Kansas City.

This is not to say that you won't find some terrific opportunities from individual mortgage brokers. You will. It's just that you can't always judge the quality and ability of the lender by the look of the Web site.

HOW DO I APPLY FOR A MORTGAGE ON-LINE?

The procedure is essentially the same as if you went to a lender's office. Of course, here you can do it from the convenience of your own home. And there are important differences, such as the opportunity to get discounts, something you would almost never get if you personally walked into a lender's office.

Here is the seven-step process. Each step is explained in detail afterward.

Seven Steps to Obtaining an E-Mortgage

Step 1   Get preapproved.

Step 2   Determine the type of mortgage you want/need.

Step 3   Check out interest rates and costs for the mortgage.

Step 4   Apply for the mortgage on-line.

Step 5   Get the documentation needed.

Step 6   Get formal approval.

Step 7   Track the mortgage until you close the deal.

Step 1. Get Preapproved

The advantage of being preapproved is twofold: first, you learn exactly how big a mortgage you can qualify for. Second, when you present an offer to a seller, once a lender has already said you can get a mortgage for a specified amount, you are a much stronger buyer than a competitor who simply thinks he or she can get a mortgage. Why not be simply prequalified?

Today, most buyers in real estate get either prequalified or preapproved. There's an important difference.

When you are prequalified, the lender asks you perhaps a dozen questions about your financial status and, based on what you say, issues a letter stating that you are qualified to get a mortgage up to a certain amount. The interest rate is also usually specified.

The prequal is really nothing more than an opinion, although coming in the form of a letter from a lender, it does carry some weight with some sellers.

When you are preapproved, you go

WARNING

With a balloon payment loan, you want to keep on your toes watching for the due date. You want to be sure you either can sell or refinance at that time.

HINT

Be sure the mortgage site gives the history of indices so you can see how volatile the mortgage rate has been in the past and is likely to be in the future.

HINT

Be sure to check that the lender offers mortgages in your area. Remember, the Internet is international in scope. You don't want to apply for a mortgage in Denver, Colorado, only to discover that the Web site is run by a local mortgage broker in Bar Harbor, Maine.

through the entire process of getting real estate financing, explained afterward, with the exception of identifying a property or getting an appraisal. The lender checks you out thoroughly, including securing a credit report and any needed documentation. Then, after all this is in, the lender issues a formal letter of preapproval. You are approved for a mortgage. This is something you can take to the bank. It's also something a seller can count on, and it makes you a far stronger buyer than one who only has a prequal letter.

Step 2. Determine the Type of Mortgage You Want/Need

There are almost more types of mortgages than there are letters in the alphabet (we'll detail many of them in Chapter 8), and they have almost as many letters in their acronyms. But most come down to two basic types: fixed interest rate and adjustable interest rate.

The fixed-rate loan is easier to understand. You pay a set monthly payment based on a set interest rate, and the loan is usually for fifteen or thirty years. The monthly payment doesn't vary (except perhaps for the very last payment, which could be a tiny bit bigger or smaller).

To muddy up the waters, however, in recent years a fixed rate with a balloon payment has come into vogue. It's a loan like the one just described whose payments are based on a thirty-year schedule, yet which also includes a due date typically at year 5, 7, or 10. Your monthly payment doesn't vary, until the last payment, which is huge, often for a large percentage of what you borrowed.

The number of adjustable rate mortgages, on the other hand, varies enormously. The interest rate, and hence the monthly payment, could change monthly, bimonthly, semiannually, annually, or at some other period of time. Furthermore, in some loans, it changes only once, in others it changes every month. (The rate is always hinged to a specific financial index.)

The mortgage lender will typically list a whole series of mortgages that it offers and you pick one. Alternatively, the lender will have a wizard that will ask you questions about your preferences and from that, select a mortgage it feels will most likely fit your needs.

Step 3. Check Out the Interest Rate and Costs for the Mortgage

A good mortgage site will list a variety of mortgages that will fit your needs. It will also show the interest rate for the mortgage as well as the costs. Scrutinize these carefully and compare them with mortgages at other Web sites.

You should look for the following:

Interest rate This is given two ways—the stated rate on the mortgage and the annual percentage rate (APR). The APR will typically be higher because it will include some charges which are paid up front. The stated rate is what your monthly payments will be based on and is what most people look at most closely. Your monthly payments will also be shown.

WARNING The monthly payments shown are usually *only* for the mortgage (principal and interest). Your actual monthly payments may also include taxes and insurance, and you'll additionally need to factor in an amount for maintenance and repairs, not to mention utilities.

Points Few consumers actually understand points. On the surface, they're deceptively easy to grasp—a point is equal to 1 percent of the loan amount and is paid up front when you get the mortgage. One point on a $125,000 mortgage, for example, comes to $1,250.

But why do lenders charge points at all?

They are charged to increase the lender's yield (return) on the mortgage (explained in Chapter 8). A lender who charges two points will be able to offer a mortgage at a slightly lower interest rate than a lender who charges no points.

Thus, when you check out the interest rate, also check out the points. You'll find that loans with zero points have higher interest rates than loans with points.

It's your choice to make. If you opt to pay points up front (typically thousands of dollars), you'll get a lower interest rate and, correspondingly, lower payments. If you opt for a zero-points loan, your interest rate and monthly payments will be somewhat higher.

Terms You can only compare apples with apples, not with persimmons. If you're looking at a fixed rate, you should compare a thirty-year loan with other thirty-year loans, not with fifteen-year loans. Because of their shorter term, *all* fifteen-year loans should carry a lower interest rate than *all* thirty-year loans (see Figure 7.2).

Similarly, all loans with a balloon payment should have a lower interest rate than thirty-year loans. For example, *all* loans with a balloon payment due in three years should have an interest

FIGURE 7.2

Comparing thirty-year fixed-rate loans.

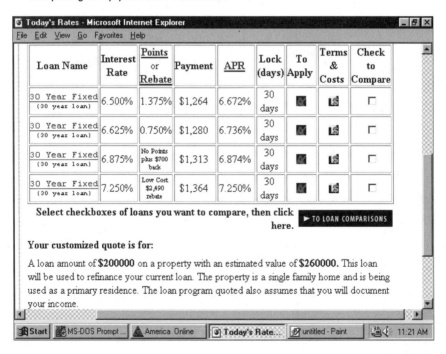

Buying a Home on the Internet

rate lower than *all* loans with a balloon payment due in seven years. *All* seven-year balloons should have an interest rate lower than *all* ten-year balloons, and so forth.

The same thing applies with adjustable mortgages. In the next chapter we'll look at the various terms. Be sure you compare loans with similar terms, or else you might think you are getting a better deal, when you are actually getting a worse one.

Garbage costs   In addition to the points, lenders also typically add on additional charges for the mortgage. These can range from document preparation to attorney fees, from administrative fees to recording fees. A good Web site will list the actual garbage costs to you. Compare them between mortgages. You may find that a mortgage that apparently has the best combination of interest rate, points, and terms, actually is less savory once you add in the garbage costs.

Why many real estate writers and I call them "garbage costs" is because most are added on to increase the yield to the lender, while presenting the illusion of a low-interest rate to the consumer. A truly straightforward lender would simply add up all the costs and factor them into the interest rate or points and charge nothing extra. But, in today's highly competitive market, most lenders, to keep that interest rate down, find they are forced to conceal the true interest rate by charging so-called garbage points. (The APR comes closest to revealing the true interest rate because it includes many, but not all, of the garbage costs that are thrown in these days.) We'll go into specific garbage costs in the next chapter.

HINT

If you've got a lot of cash, but are strapped for income, you may be wise to pay points to get a lower interest rate and payments. On the other hand, if you've got a strong income, but are cash short, then you'll probably want a zero-points loan that gets you in with less cash, but gives you higher monthly payments.

Look for other features Mortgage lenders often throw in other features that are either desirable or undesirable. For example, some lenders will *lock in* the mortgage. This means that once you've applied (and been initially qualified), they will guarantee the rate for a period of time, typically thirty or forty-five days while the deal closes. This protects you in case interest rates go up between the time you apply and the time the mortgage is funded.

On the other hand, some lenders include a prepayment penalty. This means that if you want to pay off the mortgage before it's actual due date, you have to pay a money penalty, often a large one. Even if you plan to keep the property for a long time, this is undesirable because your plans could suddenly change and you might need to sell, resulting in a money penalty. Because most lenders do not charge a prepayment penalty (as of this writing), you would be wise to seek out one that does not, all else being equal (see Figure 7.3).

FIGURE 7.3

Mortgage costs screen.

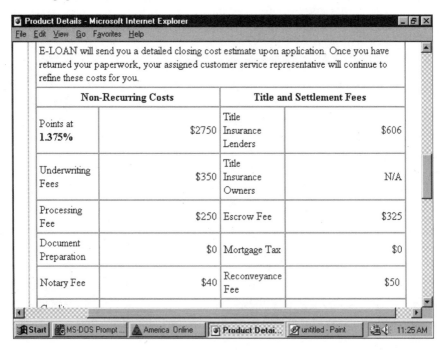

Buying a Home on the Internet

Step 4. Apply for the Mortgage On-Line

To determine if you can really get a mortgage, the lender represented by the Web site must have some confidential financial information about you. Once you've determined the type of mortgage you want, you'll need to fill out an application. The on-line application asks essentially the same questions as the physical application. It's just that you fill it out and send it in electronically.

You will also need to obtain an appraisal of the property. Although a national data bank of properties is being built so that an appraisal can be obtained electronically, it is very limited in scope as of this writing. Almost certainly, you will need to have an appraiser physically go out and examine the property. The lender will order the appraisal, but you will probably be asked to pay for it. It usually costs between $250 and $300.

How Secure Is Confidential Information Sent over the Internet?

Good question. Unfortunately, there's not really a perfect answer. There are a couple of excellent encrypting programs that are used to provide secure lines. I regularly buy items over the Internet using secure Web sites with my credit card and haven't had a problem. However, as we all know, computers are the playground of some extremely creative hackers, and who's to say that what's secure today will remain secure tomorrow?

A bigger issue, however, may be knowing with whom you are dealing. Just because someone puts up a Web site and says they are offering mortgages, doesn't necessarily mean they are doing so. After all, what's to prevent you or I from doing

HINT

On-line lenders often give discounts. It works this way: a regular mortgage broker will typically be paid 1 percent of the loan amount as a commission. You won't actually see this money, but it will be part of the interest rate/ points combination you pay. On-line lenders, however, sometimes do not charge this commission. Thus their loans may be 1 point lower or a small percentage less (perhaps $\frac{1}{2}$ of 1 percent) than if you obtained a loan by actually going to a real-site broker.

H I N T

Some e-lenders will refund the cost of the appraisal (as well as the cost of the credit report) if and when you ultimately secure a mortgage through them.

H I N T

A good mortgage Web site will explain how it secures information sent to it. Read the explanation carefully. If it doesn't make sense to you, or seems inadequate, don't send out your vital information.

just that? And then, if some poor soul gets sucked in and sends us his or her most confidential financial information, what's to prevent us from using it in a criminal way?

As far as I know, there is no regular policing of mortgage sites on the Internet. Therefore, you had best know exactly with whom you are dealing.

Obviously, you can feel more secure if you're sending information to a major bank, mortgage banker, or mortgage broker. But remember, even though the Web site may be huge and elaborate, the person who set it up may be working out of his or her bedroom and not have all the contacts that are suggested by the Web advertising.

In short, be careful. If you're not comfortable giving your most confidential information out over the Internet, don't. If you've checked out and approve of the lender, it's only a little bit more inconvenient to print out the application and send it in by mail (see Figure 7.4).

Is a Credit Report Part of the Application Process?

Lenders use a profile to determine who qualifies for what mortgage. A critical part of this profile is called your FICA (Fair Isaac) score. It is determined by an independent company that analyzes credit reports and then issues a three-digit score that lenders use. Generally speaking, a score of 700 or more will get you an "A" mortgage. Below that, you may still get a mortgage, but you might have to pay a higher interest rate, more points, or both. We'll have more to say about FICA in the next chapter.

FIGURE 7.4

Mortgage loan application screen.

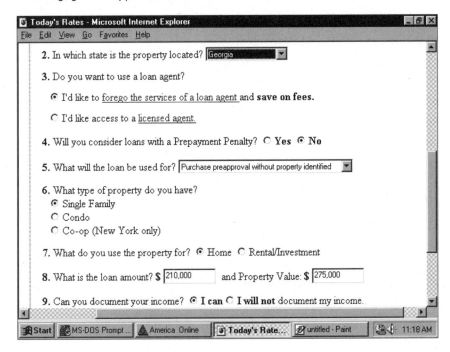

Mortgage sites will want to charge you for a credit report. As a preliminary, they will often ask for only a small fee up front, $10 to $30 for a one-bureau report. There are actually three national agencies that issue reports that mortgage lenders use and before you've completed the process, you'll need to get a three-bureau report. However, initially, many lenders will rely on the cheaper one-bureau report. Also see the note above regarding security on the Web. The credit reporting agencies are:

Trans Union   (800) 916-8800

Experion (formerly TRW)   (800) 682-7654

Equifax   (800) 685-1111

If you do all of the above on-line, the mortgage broker or lender who runs the site can get back to you within minutes telling you whether you're likely to get the e-loan you want or not. If the answer is yes, you'll be asked for documentation of what you have claimed in your application

WARNING

If the lender only wants documentation on closing, you run the risk of overlooking something or accidentally getting the wrong document. When it comes time to close and you show up with the wrong documentation, it could put the transaction on hold until you go out and get the right piece of paper, something that could take several days or longer, depending who has to sign what for you.

(see the following). If the answer is no, you will usually be offered either a lower mortgage amount, or higher interest rate/point combination.

Step 5. Get the Documentation Needed

One of the questions that you'll be asked as part of locating an appropriate loan for you is whether you are willing to supply documentation. The question refers to such things as written verification of deposit of sufficient money to handle the down payment and closing from a financial institution (such as a bank or brokerage firm), paycheck stubs and written verification of employment from your employer, W-2 forms, two years of income tax returns (if you're self-employed), and so on.

If you check that you're not willing to supply this documentation, you can still get a mortgage based on what you claim and your credit report. However, you'll likely be charged a higher interest rate, sometimes as high as from one to three points, but sometimes as low as just three-eighths of a point more, depending on how the lender sizes up your risk.

If, on the other hand, you check that you will supply documentation, then you'll get the lowest rates the lender can offer. But, you'll have to supply the documentation.

Some mortgage sites will ask for all of the documentation initially, as soon as they tell you you've qualified for the mortgage you want. Others, usually banks or mortgage bankers who fund the money themselves, may ask you to obtain the materials, but then hang onto it until closing, when you'll present it.

Either way, you have to dig up the documentation.

Step 6. Get Formal Approval

As noted earlier, most mortgage site lenders can give you approval on-line within a matter of minutes or a few hours at most. However, this approval is based on what you claim, not on what you have documented. It's usually better to ask for a formal approval, meaning the lender has all the documentation needed and is ready to fund when you need the money.

This may take several days to several weeks, depending on what kind of a mortgage you're going for and on how high-tech the lender is with whom you're dealing. Both big national underwriters who ultimately put up the money for the mortgage offer electronic underwriting with formal approval within three days or less. Not all lenders (who deal with consumers such as yourself), however, are set up to handle this, and not all types of mortgages fit the characteristics required of e-approval.

Always ask for proof of the approval. You can usually get it by e-mail, fax, or letter. I personally like the idea of a signed letter, although a fax will probably do. I don't believe an e-mail confirmation is worth much.

Step 7. Track the Mortgage Until You Close the Deal

You need to monitor the loan in progress. You should check whether the lender has received the application, whether an appraisal has been ordered, and eventually, when it has been completed, is the appraisal for enough money, what documents are you missing, and on and on.

HINT

Some mortgage lenders will continue to serve you after you get the mortgage. They will keep your mortgage and financial information in a database, and when interest rates fall, they'll call you telling you that you can save money if you refinance! Some even let you set your parameters—for example, "Call me when I can save $1000 or more. Don't bother me if I can save only a couple of hundred."

A good lender will offer you constant loan tracking. All you need do is call up the site to see what state you are in. (For example, check out "etrack" at eloan.com.) Eventually, everything will be done and you'll be ready to close.

When you're ready to close, you'll meet with an escrow officer (or attorney) who's handling the closing and sometimes with an officer of the lender. There you'll be asked to sign the application you filled out over the phone (if you didn't already do this as part of your documentation submission). If you haven't already, you'll also be asked to present any documents required, such as paycheck stub, W-2 forms, 1040 tax statements, bank statements, and so on.

If everything is as you originally represented, you will formally sign some papers and your mortgage should fund (and the house should be purchased) within a day or two. You've made it—you've gotten a mortgage electronically!

HOW LONG DOES IT TAKE?

The actual time frame can be as short as three days and as long as you need it to be. The average time is usually somewhere between three weeks and forty-five days.

If you have a specific need for a shorter or longer time frame, be sure to explain this to the person you deal with at the mortgage site. Your time frame will affect the type of mortgage you are best suited to getting as well as the lock-in period, if any.

8
CHAPTER

A MORTGAGE PRIMER

If you're new to mortgage hunting, or if it's been a while since you've obtained a new mortgage, you're sure to find your current search leading to a mind-splitting confusion of terms, loan types, and arcane procedures. "What in the world are these people thinking?" is a common reaction.

Be assured that mortgage lending does not come from another planet, although it may seem totally alien. What has happened is that over the last five years or so, the entire real estate lending process has undergone radical change and, with the proliferation of Internet borrowing, the change is continuing. What this can mean for you is benefits, but also bewilderment. Where do you start? Whom do you believe? What's going on?

In this chapter, we're going to get an overview that should help put your mind at ease. We're going to look at what you face when attempting to secure a mortgage. We'll try to make sense out of it all so that you have some idea what to expect and how to maneuver. In short, this chapter is, as its title says, a mortgage lending primer. [For a much more detailed explanation of mortgage lending, check into my *Tips & Traps When Mortgage Hunting, 2nd Edition* (McGraw-Hill, 1999).]

HOW DO LENDERS DISCRIMINATE BETWEEN BORROWERS?

In the past, to get almost any kind of mortgage you had to have good credit, a strong income, and a past history of repaying what you borrowed.

Today, it's a different story. Today, almost anyone can get a mortgage, regardless of their qualifications. However, those with the best qualifications get the lowest interest rate and the best terms, whereas those with the worst qualifications pay more and sometimes have more difficult terms. Today, there's a mortgage available for virtually everyone—just not the same mortgage.

How do mortgage lenders know who's a top, or prime, borrower and who's subprime?

HOW DO THE LENDERS SEE ME?

To begin with, you must have sufficient income to be able to handle the mortgage payments as well as a large down payment. In the past lenders looked at your income and your expenses. If you had sufficient income, after expenses, to make the mortgage payments plus taxes, insurance, utilities, and maintenance (according to specific formulas), you basically qualified (as long as you had a decent credit report).

However, we're living in the new world of computers, which are able to analyze huge amounts of data. What lenders (here, we're referring to major secondary lenders who ultimately finance most U.S. residential real estate, Fannie Mae, and Freddie Mac) discovered was that the old formulas were not all that reliable in terms of predicting future performance. Some borrowers who looked great would end up defaulting after only a few months, whereas others who seemed marginal would never miss a payment.

To try to separate the wheat from the chaff, these lenders began examining the past performance of borrowers based on factors other than (or in addition to) the traditional ones. They considered such items as the total past history of payments, the number of trade accounts (credit cards), how long the borrower had used credit cards, how much money the borrower held in reserve, and on and on.

By examining hundreds of thousands of past borrowers, the lenders put together a profile of what a worthy borrower would look like. Today, that profile determines whether you can get an A loan, or whether you have to get a lesser mortgage.

ARE YOU A PRIME BORROWER?

When you apply for a mortgage, you'll be asked to fill out a questionnaire that has about sixty items on it. It will cover a broad range of questions about your financial condition as well as your borrowing history. After filling out the questionnaire, the mortgage broker (who takes your application) will secure a credit report and from the information thus gathered, you'll be given a score.

Scoring is done by several organizations, the largest of which is Fair Isaac. This private agency takes a look at your credit history and comes up with a three-digit score. Typically, if you score above 680, you'll probably qualify for a prime mortgage. If your score is below, you may have to get a lesser mortgage.

It's important to understand that scoring is arbitrary and little things can mean a lot. For example, if you apply for credit more than three times in a six-month period, it could lower your score. If you have more than three new credit cards, it could lower your score. On the other hand, if you have loads of money in the bank in reserve, it could raise your score. If you put more money down (say 30 percent), it could raise your score astronomically. Many people are simply amazed at the score they get, for good or bad.

Prime borrowers are those who have virtually no credit problems, strong income, and lots of cash in the bank. They are also called A borrowers. Everyone else is subprime and is rated from A– down to D.

Here's a chart to help you see how you rate. Note: this chart just rates your credit, not your income/expenses. Also, these are unofficial guidelines—each lender has its own yardstick. [Chart courtesy of *Tips & Traps When Mortgage Hunting, 2nd Edition* (McGraw-Hill, 1999).]

What Kind of a Borrower Are You?

Rating	Description
A	Most creditworthy. Fit underwriter's profile.
A–	One bill, under $1000, turned into collection or no more than one late payment of over sixty days or two late payments of over thirty days in credit cards or installment debt all within the last two years.
B	Within the past year and a half you have up to four late payments of no more than thirty days in credit cards or installment debt. You may have had a bankruptcy or foreclosure concluded at least two years before applying for loan.
C	Within the past year you have up to six late payments of no more than thirty days in credit cards or installment debt. You may have accounts currently in collection, but

mortgage may be granted if they are no more than $5000 and paid in full by the time the mortgage is funded. Mortgage funds may be used to clean up these debts. If you have a bankruptcy, it was resolved at least a year before applying for the mortgage. If you had a foreclosure, it was concluded at least two years before applying for loan.

D You have many current late payments, have several accounts in collection, and have judgments against you. These can be paid off from the proceeds of the new mortgage. If you have a bankruptcy, it was concluded more than six months before you applied for the new mortgage. If you had a foreclosure, it was concluded at least two years before applying for the loan.

WHAT DOES IT MEAN TO ME IF I AM A PRIME BORROWER?

It means that you can get a "conforming" loan. A conforming loan is one that will pass the underwriting standards of the two big secondary lenders, Fannie Mae and Freddie Mac. It's important to understand that the company that actually lends you the money will most likely subsequently "sell" your mortgage to one of the big two to get its money back so that it can relend it again. Of importance to you is that with a conforming loan you'll be getting a mortgage at the lowest possible interest rate and points.

Most of the companies that offer mortgages on-line are actually offering conforming loans. If it turns out that you're not a prime borrower (A– or lower), they may not be able to help you get a mortgage, but may instead refer you to other lenders.

WHAT IS A CONFORMING LOAN?

A conforming loan has certain requirements. For example, usually you must intend to occupy the property as your personal residence. You must be a prime borrower to qualify. And, the loan has a maximum amount, which is raised periodically. As of this writing, the maximum is $227,150.

WHAT DOES IT MEAN IF I'M A SUBPRIME BORROWER?

It's important to understand that you can still get a mortgage. You'll just have to pay more. If you're an A– or B borrower, that could amount to as little as 0.5 percent more. On the other hand, if you're a C or D borrower, it could be several percent more—perhaps 4 or 5 percent higher than for a prime borrower.

There are many institutional lenders such as banks and mortgage bankers who have programs for subprime borrowers. There are also many credit companies that specialize in the subprime borrower. Today, getting a mortgage is a matter of how much you're willing and able to pay. If you are a subprime borrower, it can just mean that you have to put up a bigger down payment, or accept a higher interest rate and monthly payment, and you probably can't get an on-line loan.

WHAT IF NO ONE WILL LEND TO ME?

Even if you have terrible credit, today you can still get financing of one sort or another. You may be able to "assume" or take over an existing mortgage. Some older FHA (Federal Housing Administration) and VA (Veterans Administration) mortgages require no qualifying.

You may be able to get equity financing, in which the lender really doesn't care a wit about you, but only about the property. Here the maximum loan is usually for only 70 percent of the property's value, but there is, again, no qualifying. The interest rate and points, however, are typically higher.

You may be able to get seller financing. Here the seller carries the "paper," or mortgage. Many sellers are willing to do this if the market is soft and they're having a hard time selling. Check with a good real estate agent about the possibilities.

WHAT KINDS OF MORTGAGES ARE AVAILABLE TO ME?

These days there are more mortgages available than you can shake a stick at. We've touched on a couple above, however, here's a list for the types you're likely to find on-line and a brief explanation to help you decide what might be most suitable for you.

What Is a 125-Percent Mortgage?

It's a mortgage for *more* than the value of your property. Mortgages are collateralized loans—that means that their security is first the property. That's why traditionally mortgages have always been for a percentage of the property's market value, typically 80 or 90 percent. How, therefore, can a lender make a loan for 125 percent, far more than the market value of the property?

In most cases, the 125-percent loan is actually two mortgages—a collateralized mortgage based on a percentage of the property's value, and then a second uncollateralized loan based on the good credit of the borrower. It works like this: a very high mortgage is obtained, between 90 and 100 percent of the property value. Then added to the mortgage is, in effect, a personal (noncollateralized) loan for an additional 25 to 35 percent. The combination of the two gives a total loan of 125 percent of market value.

Of course, the loan may specify only one payment to a lender. The lender then separates your payment into two parts, one for the personal loan and the remainder for the mortgage.

The interest rate is a combination of the two loans. It may be quite low on the collateralized portion, higher on the personal portions. However, the combined rate may only be a percentage point or two higher than for a conforming loan.

Always keep in mind that with a 125-percent mortgage, you have no equity in the property. If you want to sell (or resell), you'll find it next to impossible. You will owe 25 percent more than the property's worth—you have negative equity. A job change, a medical problem, or an income loss could come along suddenly and demand that you move; however, your ability to get rid of the property and move would be crippled by the loans.

Also, you probably won't be able to deduct the interest on at least the personal portion of the mortgage (something the lender may not mention).

What Is an ARM?

In an adjustable rate mortgage (ARM), the interest rate and payment fluctuate over the term of the loan. Because it often carries a lower initial interest rate, this type of loan is most frequently used when interest rates are high and the borrower needs a lower rate to qualify for a mortgage. It's also useful when you're only going to keep the mortgage for a short time (you're planning to resell the property) and want a lower interest rate during that period.

What Is a Teaser?

To induce borrowers to go with their ARM, lenders usually offer a *teaser*. When a borrower asks how much the ARM's interest rate is, he or she is usually told the teaser rate, which may be as much as three points less than the current market rate. For example, the teaser rate may be 5 percent, whereas the market rate for fixed mortgages is 8 percent. This is usually quite an inducement to borrowers to consider the ARM, who otherwise would probably go for a fixed interest rate.

What Are the Margin and Index?
To determine the actual interest rate you will pay on an ARM, there are two factors to consider: the underlying index and the margin. The index reflects the cost of borrowing money to lenders based on a particular market (for example, one year T-Bills, the average cost of funds to lenders, or some other well-known and easily accessible rate).

The lender then adds a specific margin to the index, say 3 percent. Thus, if the index happens to be 5 percent on a given day and the margin is 3 percent, your interest rate would be the combination of the two, or 8 percent. Note that while the index fluctuates, the margin does not.

What Is the Adjustment Period?
After the index, the next critical feature to look at in an ARM is the adjustment period. How frequently can the lender adjust the mortgage rate up or down?

The adjustment period for a given loan is arbitrary, and each lender will specify what it wants in the loan documents. However, different lenders and even the same lender will offer different loans with different adjustment periods. Therefore, for the borrower, this is something you can pick and choose. Some of the more common adjustment periods are monthly, every six months, and once a year.

It's usually to your advantage to get the longest adjustment period possible. This gives you the greatest stability. On the other hand, lenders want the shortest adjustment period. This gives them the greatest protection against interest rate hikes.

What Are Caps?
One of the biggest problems with ARMs is the uncertainty that they produce. The borrower never really knows what the interest rate and, hence, his or her payments are going to be tomorrow. It's this uncertainty that causes many borrowers to forego ARMs.

Lenders are aware of borrowers' fears of hikes in mortgage payments caused by unlimited interest rate hikes on ARMs. To help reduce borrowers' fears, lenders frequently put *caps,* or limits, on the ARM. They limit either the amount the interest rate can rise (or fall), the amount the monthly payment can rise, or both.

Are Caps a Good Thing?

Although most borrowers would agree that interest rate caps are beneficial, they can be deceptive. They don't really give as much protection as they seem to. The reason is that they are set so high. Often for them to kick in, interest rates would have to reach historical highs, and that's unlikely. Caps are more protection for the long shot, rather than for month-to-month payments.

Some ARMs also set a maximum limit on the amount the monthly payment (a payment cap) can be raised each adjustment period, regardless of what happens to the interest rate. This has an unusual and profound effect on the mortgage. Interest, which is charged against the mortgage, cannot be paid because the payment is not high enough to accommodate it. Therefore, the excess interest is added to the mortgage principal.

It's called negative amortization or interest on interest. Most government underwritten mortgages allow up to 25 percent of the original mortgage amount to be added interest. In other words, you can end up owing 125 percent of what you borrowed because of negative amortization.

Does your mortgage have negative amortization? It is something that is often hidden from view, unless you know what to look for in the documents. Although the negative amortization terms are usually explained in those mortgages in which it occurs, many people simply don't understand the implications. It means, quite simply, that if interest rates rise rapidly, the amount you owe may rise as well. You could end up owing far more than you originally borrowed!

What Are Interest Rate Steps?

Many ARMs set a maximum limit on the amount the interest can be raised each adjustment period. Regardless of what the real interest rate has moved, the interest rate on the mortgage with steps can only be adjusted upward (or downward) at predetermined amounts, say 1 or 2 percent. For example, let's say your adjustment period is every six months, and during the latest six-month period, interest rates have jumped 3 percent. If your step is 1 percent, your interest rate couldn't go up more than 1 percent during the current adjustment period. (However, it could rise an additional 1 percent the next period and the one after that to eventually rise to market rate.)

Nearly all ARMs have steps that limit the hikes in the interest rate per each adjustment period. These limits are typically anywhere from 0.5 percent to 2.5 percent per adjustment period. Thus, regardless of what the index the mortgage is tied to may do, the interest rate cannot be hiked more than the step amount each period.

Keep in mind that the smaller the steps, the greater the lag time when there is a sudden jump in your interest rate. (Of course, a sudden decline would not be felt as quickly, either.) Ideally, you would want a mortgage with small steps over one with larger ones.

What Is a Balloon Mortgage?

Balloon in real estate finance means nothing more than to have one payment of a mortgage (usually the last) be larger than all of the others. For example, you might get a second mortgage for $10,000, which is all due and payable in three years. During the three-year period, you might pay interest only. If the interest were 6 percent, you'd owe $50 a month. However, at the end of the three years, you'd owe the full $10,000 back. (Remember, you were paying interest *only.*) That last payment would be considered a balloon.

Any mortgage can incorporate a balloon in it. One of the most popular mortgages as of this writing is the 7/30. In this mortgage, the payments are amortized, or spread out, over thirty years. However, the entire mortgage is due in seven years. In other words, you make payments as if the mortgage was for thirty years. However, at the end of year seven, the remaining balance all comes due and payable.

The result for you is a lower monthly payment. For the lender, this type of loan means less exposure to interest rate changes, because the amount borrowed is only for seven years. In exchange for the shorter payoff period, lenders typically offer a slightly better interest rate. For example, the 7/30 may mean you'll pay one-quarter to three-eighths less interest than the straight thirty.

Lenders can be quite creative with balloons. The loan can be a 3/30, 5/30, or 10/30. The interest rate, correspondingly, will be lower for the shorter the term, higher for longer.

Balloon payments are also often found when there is seller financing. As noted earlier, the loan may be interest only, something sellers are inclined to offer with a balloon payment at the end. Home equity financing also tends to employ balloons.

Be wary of mortgages with balloons. When they come due, you need to have the money to pay them off. That may mean you need to be able to either sell the property or refinance. It's usually a good idea to insist on a clause in a balloon mortgage that provides for an automatic refinance (even if it's at a higher interest rate) at the balloon, just in case.

What Is a Biweekly Mortgage?

In a biweekly mortgage, the borrower makes a payment every other week instead of the traditional once-monthly payment. Because there are fifty-two weeks in the year, a payment every other week results in twenty-six half payments, or thirteen full payments. With a biweekly mortgage, therefore, each year you make the equivalent of thirteen monthly payments instead of twelve.

By making an extra payment each year, which goes to principal, over the life of the loan an amazing amount of interest is saved. As a result, the mortgage can be paid off years earlier. In almost a painless way, you can cut almost a third off the time it takes to pay off a thirty-year mortgage.

The biweekly mortgage allows many people to painlessly and effortlessly increase their principal payments. However, keep in mind that a biweekly mortgage is not for everyone. It works best when you are salaried, getting paid on a weekly or biweekly basis. You can easily budget your money to take care of the payment that way and probably won't feel the extra expense very much. On the other hand, if you're paid monthly or work for yourself, the biweekly setup can be a disaster for you. You won't have the money handy on a biweekly schedule.

The time to establish a biweekly mortgage is when you first get financing. Look for a lender that will set the program up for you; not all lenders will do this.

If you already have a mortgage or find a lender who won't do this for you, be sure your mortgage contains no prepayment penalty (described later) clause and then set it up for yourself. It couldn't be easier. Every two weeks simply deposit half the mortgage payment into a checking account. Then once a month pay your mortgage payment from this account. (This can be set up electronically with some banks so that the deposit in will automatically come from your paycheck, and the payments out will automatically go to the lender.)

At the end of a year, you should have the equivalent of an extra month's worth of payments in the account. Now, simply send this to the lender specifying that it must go to principal, not interest. (If you don't specify this, the lender very likely will just consider it the next monthly payment.) You've added the equivalent of a monthly payment's worth to your principal and have made a significant step toward paying down your mortgage.

Of course, there are companies that will do this for you for a fee. However, why pay someone else to do what you can easily do for yourself, as noted above.

What Is a Fast Mortgage?

If you are a prime borrower, you may be able to get a mortgage in less than three days, including funding. This is incredibly fast, because the typical mortgage takes between thirty and forty-five days to secure.

Fast mortgages are basically conforming loans. They are underwritten through the Loan Prospector program of Freddie Mac and several programs of Fannie Mae. They are handled primarily by computer.

Many mortgage brokers, including some who are on-line, can handle these types of mortgages. Basically, the procedure is essentially the same as for any mortgage. You fill out an application, a credit report is secured, you are scored, and if you meet the profile requirements, the underwriter indicates you will be approved. It's then a matter of getting a mortgage lender to move quickly.

When asking about a mortgage, whether in person or on-line, ask specifically for *automated mortgage underwriting.* If the lender with whom you're dealing doesn't know what you're talking about, go to a different on-line lender.

What About a Fixed-Rate Mortgage?

This is the traditional mortgage that has helped finance residential real estate for over the past seventy years. The interest rate is fixed at the time you get the mortgage and does not vary over its term. If it starts out at 7 percent for thirty years, that's what it remains over the entire 360 payments.

The advantage of the fixed-rate mortgage is that you always know what your payment is going to be. Because the interest rate is fixed, so too is the payment. Furthermore, if interest rates in the market rise, you're not going to be affected. Your rate will remain the same.

The disadvantage is that the interest rate for a fixed-rate mortgage tends to be higher than for the ARM alternative. However, in a stable or even a falling market, the differential typically is low. There's usually only a big advantage to an ARM in terms of interest rates when the market rate is rising.

In general, the time to go for a fixed-rate loan is when interest rates are low. You lock in the low rate. When interest rates are high, an ARM may be a better alternative, particularly if it includes an option that allows you to switch (without additional cost) after a period of time to a fixed rate. (Some ARMS offer a switch window at year three or five of the mortgage.)

What About Government-Insured or Guaranteed Loans?

The Veteran's Administration (VA) has a guaranteed loan program and the Federal Housing Administration (FHA) offers an insured program. Neither of these agencies actually loans money, but instead either guarantees or insures to the lender a mortgage that you obtain (in the event you default on the payments).

Qualifications are stringent. In terms of the VA, you must have been a veteran during certain, specific time periods. (Check with the VA for the current time periods.) For the FHA, you must qualify almost as rigorously as for a conforming loan (be a prime borrower).

The advantage of these mortgages is the low down payment or, in the case of a VA loan, no down payment. The disadvantage, at least in the past, has been the low mortgage amount, although this may have risen to the same as for conforming loans by the time you read this.

In the past these loans have been assumable, with a catch—unless the person who assumed a VA loan was also a veteran, you remained liable for repayment, even if the person you sold the property to didn't make the payments! Recently, FHA loans have become more difficult to assume, with the new borrower required to qualify as if it were for a new loan.

Additionally, with lower down payments required for some conventional loans, the advantages of these government program mortgages has diminished. These loans are harder to arrange on-line.

What About a Home Equity Mortgage?

There's really not much difference between a home equity loan and a second mortgage. The term *home equity* is actually a marketing slogan that banks and other lenders use to induce property owners to borrow money on their homes.

Home equity loans can be used for virtually any purpose, from college education for the kids to fixing up the property. Usually the lenders don't care. (There are some specific fix-up loans available through the FHA that require they be used to improve or remodel property.)

The interest on home equity loans can usually be deducted, up to certain limits (often a $100,000 loan maximum). There are other conditions as well, so check with a good accountant before assuming your home equity mortgage interest is fully deductible from your taxes.

Some home equity loans are actually revolving lines of credit, much like a credit card. The loan is set up for a specific amount of money, say $100,000. Then you borrow against it and pay only interest monthly. At any time you can pay down on the principal without penalty. Usually these have a maximum lending period of ten years after which you can no longer borrow but must instead pay back the existing balance over a twenty-year period.

The interest rate on home equity loans is typically a couple of points higher than for conforming first mortgages.

For quick credit, you can't beat a home equity loan. Once set up, they're in place whenever you need them. Instead of having to borrow cash at very high interest rates (often 20 percent or more) on credit cards, you can borrow it on the home equity loan, typically for half that amount.

Keep in mind, however, that to get this type of financing, you must have considerable equity in your property. Generally speaking, your combined mortgages (first plus home equity) cannot exceed 80 percent of the property value. Look for an on-line bank.

What Is a Jumbo Mortgage?

What if you live in a high-priced area, such as parts of New York or California? What if the average home in your area costs over $300,000 or, in some cases, over $500,000? How do you get financing?

The answer is a *jumbo loan.* If you need a mortgage above the conforming limitation, you operate under a different set of rules.

Some mortgage brokers, savings banks, or other on-line lenders offer jumbos. The procedure for getting one is essentially the same as for a regular mortgage: fill out an application, provide the required documentation, get an appraisal, and if everything checks out, get approval.

What's different is who offers the mortgage. With conforming loans, the lender funds the mortgage, then resells it to a secondary lender (Fannie Mae or Freddie Mac). With a jumbo, generally speaking, the lender keeps the mortgage itself in its own portfolio. That's why these are often called *portfolio loans.*

Jumbos are readily available in those areas of the country where they are needed. However, they tend to cost about one-half a percentage point higher in interest. And, you must still be a prime borrower to qualify for one.

A hybrid version of the jumbo is the *piggyback.* Here you get two loans: the first a conforming loan up to the maximum amount allowed, then a second mortgage that goes the rest of the way up to the money limit you need. The interest rate on these loans is a blend of the conforming rate and the higher jumbo rate, which usually means a combined, slightly lower interest rate and payment for you than a straight jumbo. Of course, you only make one monthly payment, the lender separating out the amount that goes to the conforming loan and the portion that goes to the jumbo.

A jumbo can be either a fixed rate or an ARM. It can be one of the popular 7/30 or 10/30 balloon mortgages or a fully amortized fixed rate. The big difference with a jumbo is the amount borrowed.

What Is a Low- or No-Document Mortgage?

If you're self-employed, you may find that it's somewhat more difficult to get financing. The basic reason is that it is usually more difficult for you to document all of the income you make. An employed person need only show a W-2 form and a paycheck stub to verify income received from an employer. A self-employed person, however, typically must show two years' worth of federal tax returns, and in some cases, these returns may not show all income.

One option for those who are self-employed (and for anyone else who has difficulty in verifying income) is a low-document mortgage. These loans simply do not require much documentation. Typically, there are no verifications from employers or banks, perhaps no tax returns, and usually only a credit report is required.

There is simply an application and a statement to be signed by the borrower, which says, upon penalty of perjury, that he or she made as much money as was claimed. Based on that statement, a mortgage is issued.

If you opt for a low-doc mortgage, and you make the payments as promised, everything should be fine. However, if for some reason you can't make the payments, it could mean big trouble. If the mortgage goes into foreclosure, then the government may investigate and you may have to prove that you indeed did have all the income you claimed. If you didn't, at the time the mortgage was issued, then you could be guilty of fraud, for which there are severe penalties.

In addition, a low-doc mortgage often carries a somewhat higher interest rate, and you could be required to come up with a larger down payment—25 percent instead of the usual 10 or 20 percent. Finally, there may be more points to pay than for a documented mortgage.

In the past, there was an even more lenient type of mortgage to qualify for called a no-documentation loan. All that was required was the sworn statement of the borrower. However, because of excessive defaults, this type of loan is seldom offered today.

For the self-employed individual who has trouble showing as much income as he or she actually makes, a low-doc mortgage can be a godsend. It gives you the opportunity to get a mortgage to buy a home on little more than your signature and good credit. These are available on-line from some lenders.

What Is a Zero-Points Mortgage?

Most mortgages carry points. As described in greater detail later, a point is interest equal to 1 percent of the amount borrowed. Thus, a $100,000 mortgage at three points carries an extra fee of $3000.

Lenders charge points to increase their yield on the mortgage. The points are added in with the interest rate when computing the overall return. When you are given the annual percentage rate (APR) as computed by the government, it includes points (as well as some other fees.)

A zero-points mortgage, therefore, is one in which the lender charges you no points at all. In other words, there is no additional interest to pay beyond the rate for the loan.

How can lenders offer zero-points mortgages? It's done by jacking up the interest rate. You want to borrow $100,000 at 8 percent, and the lender says it will cost you two points. But, you don't want to pay two points; you don't want to pay any points.

The lender agrees and says, "Okay, you don't have to pay any points, only now the interest rate is $8\frac{1}{4}$ percent." It will allow you to trade points for a higher interest rate. In today's market place, trading points for interest has become commonplace. If you do make such a trade, however, try to be sure that you don't pay an excessively high interest rate to get your points reduced. (A rule of thumb is that one point is usually equal to about one-eighth of 1 percent in interest, although this does not hold up in all cases. In point of fact, the actual trade-off relates to yield—the yield should be the same either for a lower interest rate with points or a higher interest rate without. A good mortgage broker can quickly calculate this for you.)

WHAT ARE THE PITFALLS TO WATCH OUT FOR?

When looking for a mortgage on-line, there are a number of areas of concern. We'll cover several here, the first of which is excessive fees.

Watch Out for Garbage Fees

Over the past few years, all lenders have found themselves in a highly competitive market. They know that borrowers will shop around for mortgages. Therefore, to keep their interest rates and points low, they have begun adding fees. These fees add to the yield of a mortgage, but because they are often overlooked (at least initially by the borrowers), they can be added with less of a problem than raising the interest rate or adding points.

Some fees are justified. For example, there is a legitimate recording fee (paid to the county) that someone must pay when the mortgage is obtained. It's only reasonable that the borrower pay it.

Most fees, however, are just garbage. These include charges for lender's attorney, drawing up documents, securing underwriting, and so on. These are fees that occur in the normal course of doing business as a lender. They ought to be included in the overall cost of the mortgage—the interest rate and points. However, they are almost always sneaked in as additional fees that you must pay.

Can you get out of paying the garbage fees? Not anymore. A few years ago, you could shop around for lenders that didn't charge them. However, I recently was searching for a lender who didn't charge garbage fees and couldn't find one anywhere in the country! That doesn't mean one doesn't exist, just that if I couldn't find it, you may not be able to, either.

The garbage fees often amount to $1000 or more. Just count on that as extra charges when you get your mortgage.

By the way, all lenders are required to give you a fair estimate of costs and fees at the time you apply under the Real Estate Settlement Procedures Act (RESPA). However, in recent years lenders have become aware of the fact that there is virtually no governmental enforcement of

RESPA, hence the "errors" on these estimates have sometimes been huge. It could turn out that the final garbage fees are thousands more than on the estimate. If that's the case, I would complain, and generally speaking, most lenders will do something to correct the problem. However, don't expect it to be corrected automatically.

Watch Out for a Prepayment Penalty

A prepayment penalty simply means that when you pay off your mortgage ahead of its normal due date, you must pay the lender a penalty for the privilege. For example, your loan is for ten years, but after three years, you sell the property. If you have a prepayment penalty, you will owe the lender a penalty for early payment. This penalty could be substantial, often running into many thousands of dollars.

The history of the prepayment penalty is interesting. Decades ago there was always a prepayment penalty on mortgages, typically six months worth of interest. The idea was that the prepayment penalty encouraged borrowers to keep the loan on the property when they sold. (Such loans were also typically assumable.)

With the high inflation and high interest rates of the late 1970s and 1980s, however, lenders wanted to discourage borrowers from holding onto existing, often low–interest rate, mortgages. They wanted them paid off and replaced with high-interest loans. So lenders did away with both the prepayment penalty and assumability.

More recently, however, some lenders have brought back the prepayment penalty (though not loan assumability). This was instituted during the period in the mid to late 1990s when interest rates were falling and borrowers frequently would refinance mortgages that were only a few months old. The rapid refinancing of mortgages meant that lenders were reprocessing loans too frequently and, hence, were losing money.

Today, you usually can choose between on-line lenders that offer prepayment penalties and those that don't. All else being equal, my suggestion is that you avoid the prepayment penalty. It benefits only the lender, not you.

Note: Prepayment penalties are becoming much more common among second mortgage, particularly home equity, loans. Also, if you must accept a prepayment penalty, try to get one for the lowest amount possible and with a specific termination date. For example, some such penalties expire after you've held the mortgage for three years or so, a definite plus over a penalty that remains for the entire loan period.

What's the Difference: A Mortgage Broker Versus a Mortgage Banker?

The difference is subtle, but important. An on-line mortgage broker is an individual or company that is licensed as a real estate agent with specific authority to broker mortgages. A broker goes out and finds lenders and then connects these lenders with you, a prospective borrower. For this service the broker receives a fee from the lender.

Mortgage brokers are also sometimes called retailers. The reason is that they retail mortgages. They deal directly with consumers. Many lenders, such as banks, don't want the cost of establishing lending offices around the state or the country, so they rely, instead, on mortgage brokers. A broker might be a retailer for dozens of different lenders. Because of his or her broad source of funds, the mortgage broker can often come up with a loan that will fit your specific needs.

An on-line mortgage banker, on the other hand, also sometimes deals directly with consumers. But the mortgage banker is also the lender. It uses its own funds to loan money to you. (Then typically pools a group of mortgages together and resells them on the secondary market to Fannie Mae, Freddie Mac, or another secondary lender.)

A mortgage banker will normally only be able to offer you the various types of mortgages that it specifically has. In other words, you can't shop with different lenders when you're dealing with a mortgage banker.

When you shop for a mortgage on the Internet, you'll run across both mortgage bankers and mortgage brokers. You can usually tell them apart because the mortgage brokers will offer you loans from a wide variety of loan types from many different lenders (for example, lender XYZ, lender NorthSouth, lender Quick&Friendly, and so forth). The mortgage banker will only offer you different types of loans (for example, a fixed-rate, an ARM, a hybrid, and so forth), but no mention of other lenders.

Money is money and you should shop for the best deal you can get. Just remember, however, both mortgage brokers and mortgage bankers on the Internet are able to cut their fees when you borrow on-line, because they aren't paying for a storefront or other retail costs, and this should benefit you.

What Are Points and Why Should I Pay Them?

We've already discussed this somewhat, but a closer look is worthwhile, considering the fact that you may have to pay thousands of dollars in points when you get your mortgage.

A point, as noted earlier, is equal to 1 percent of a mortgage. Let's be sure we understand this. Let's say we have a mortgage for $200,000:

1 point = $2000
2 points = $4000
3 points = $6000
½ point = $1000
¾ point = $1500

As you can see, the cost for points can add up quite quickly. But why have points at all? Why do lenders charge them when they already are charging interest?

The answer has mostly to do with marketing. Lenders want to be able to say they are offering a lower–interest rate mortgage than their competitors. But, because the cost of funds is roughly the same for all lenders, the interest rate is also roughly the same. Therefore, some lenders decided that they would charge prepaid interest (interest paid in advance at the time you obtain your mortgage) and then subtract that prepaid interest from the interest paid over the term of the loan. In that way, their advertised interest rate would be lower than the market rate. That prepaid interest is points.

When you add the points to the interest rate (plus the garbage fees noted earlier), you get the true yield of the mortgage. At any given time, the true yield of any mortgage from any lender (given an equally qualified property and borrower) is going to be roughly the same.

This is the reason that many lenders these days will trade off between points and interest rate. Pay fewer points and get a higher interest rate (and monthly payments). Pay more points and get a lower interest rate (and lower monthly payments).

I'm sure that some readers are wondering what the exact ratio between points and interest rate is? Is it that one point actually is equivalent to ⅛ percent in interest? ¼ percent? 1/16 percent?

Actually, the calculation involves a complex formula that requires us to know the yield the lender wants. Furthermore, some lenders skew the results favoring either borrowers who want a higher interest rate or borrowers who are willing to pay more points. In other words, the relationship between points and interest rate actually fluctuates depending on the specific mortgage you are going after and the lender.

As if all this isn't complex enough, some points aren't prepaid interest at all. For example, some mortgages have an origination fee, which might be anywhere from ½ to 1½ points. This is a fee that the lender collects for the privilege of giving you the mortgage. Because it is a fee, it's not prepaid interest (although the lender may calculate it into its own formula for determining yield) and could be deductible from your income taxes.

Some points are deductible from your income taxes in the year you pay them and some must be amortized over the entire loan period. Other conditions apply, such as whether the property is your personal residence. It wouldn't hurt to check with an accountant to see whether any points you pay are immediately deductible.

9
CHAPTER

SHOULD I HAVE THE HOME INSPECTED?

What if someone walked up to you and said, "I have a Rolex watch here that I can sell to you for a hundred and fifty bucks." You're not an expert on watches, but you're pretty sure a Rolex costs thousands of dollars, many thousands. I would guess that your tendency is to scoff at the offer. After all, why would someone give you such a bargain. But then again, maybe that person is desperate and needs cash. Maybe it's a legitimate offer. You could be passing up a chance to score big. The real question is, how do you know? How do you know if you're looking at pearls or swine ears?

The answer, of course, is to call in an expert. Find someone who knows watches and have him or her tell you if it's a genuine Rolex. If it is, then buy it. If not, then all you've wasted is whatever you had to offer the expert for the appraisal. And if the seller refuses to let you call in an expert? Well, that speaks volumes for itself, doesn't it?

It's no different when buying a home. If you're about to pay hundreds of thousands of dollars (considerably more than for any watch) for a piece of property, you'd better know exactly what you're getting. After all, the price is predicated on a certain level of quality. If the quality isn't there, then you're paying too high a price.

WHAT ABOUT SELLER'S DISCLOSURES?

In about half the states sellers are required to disclose any defects they know about in the house. (In the other half, most sellers do it anyway, to protect themselves from buyers later saying they were cheated.)

You should check the disclosures carefully. After reading them, you may decide you actually don't want to buy the property. (Some states allow you to back out of the deal gracefully within a set number of days, if you disapprove the disclosures.)

What's important to understand is that disclosures do not take the place of an inspection. The seller may not know of a serious defect, hence not disclose it; or, the seller may simply neglect to mention something defective he or she knows about. Yet, an inspection could turn it up. This could influence your decision on whether to buy as well as result in a renegotiated price favoring you. You need both disclosures and an inspection.

WILL AN INSPECTION REALLY INFLUENCE THE PRICE?

Okay, you may be thinking, so I'll get the place inspected. But, what's the big deal? How much can the inspection actually influence the price I'd pay for the home? A few hundred dollars? A few thousand?

It can be a whole lot more than that. Let's say you're buying a home on-line for $200,000. You've looked at the property and it appears to be in good shape, as far as you can tell. The paint isn't chipped, the carpeting seems clean and fairly new—in short, you feel you're getting a home in reasonably good condition and, as such, it's worth the purchase price.

But, let's say further that the home is really hiding all sorts of severe problems. These include the following:

The roof leaks and needs to be replaced.	$12,000
Corroded galvanized pipes need to be replaced by copper.	7,000
The foundation is badly cracked and must be fixed.	25,000
The water heater leaks and a new one is needed.	350
Total mandatory repair work	44,350

If you knew of these problems, would you still be willing to pay $200,000? Anything close to that amount?

I certainly wouldn't. I would reduce my offer by a minimum of $44,350, probably more, considering I would have to oversee the repair work. I might only offer $150,000 for the same property. It really isn't worth more because of the defects.

An inspection could turn up nothing. Or it could turn up tens of thousands of dollars worth of problems. An inspection lets you know how much to deduct from apparent market value for defects. If there are none, then you can pay full price. If there are some or many, you will want to reduce your price accordingly.

Remember, unless you're an expert in the field, it's very unlikely that you can determine if the roof leaks, if there are corroded galvanized pipes, if the foundation is broken, even if the water heater needs to be replaced, or if there are other serious problems. Most people simply can't locate the major defects just by walking through a home a few times.

You need the expert. Just as you would want an expert to tell you if it really was a Rolex, you need an expert to tell you what problems, if any, exist in the home you're buying. Remember, the price you offer, indeed your very decision to purchase, hinges on the condition of the property. (We'll have more to say later in this chapter about how to renegotiate the price if the inspection reveals serious problems.)

WHEN SHOULD I HAVE THE INSPECTION?

The usual procedure is to find the property, make an offer that contains an inspection contingency clause, and then, only after the seller has accepted the offer, order the inspection.

There's no point in ordering an inspection until you and the seller have agreed on price and terms. The inspection itself costs

HINT

A contingency clause is one in which the purchase is *subject to* the fulfillment of some action. In this case, your purchase would be subject to your approval of a home inspection report, typically within 10 to 15 days. If you don't approve the report, you don't have to buy and you get your deposit back. Be sure a competent agent or attorney writes in the clause so that it's effective.

several hundred dollars and if you haven't got a deal sewed up, it could simply be money wasted. The contingency clause protects you in case the report reveals defects (you can get out of the deal or renegotiate it).

What if the Seller Already Had the Property Inspected?

WARNING

A seller refusing to allow an inspection suggests a hidden problem may exist. Furthermore, were you to buy without an inspection because the seller refused to have it, and if later on some hidden defect turned up, the seller might be held liable. In other words, in today's litigious society, no sensible seller will refuse to allow a buyer to have a property inspection or reinspection.

Occasionally, you'll find that the seller of the property has already had the property inspected. These days, sellers are well aware that buyers will want an inspection and that, if something's amiss, it can cause a reduction in price, require expensive repairs, or lose the deal. To head this off, sellers sometimes order an inspection prior to putting their property up for sale. Then, if something is found that requires fixing, the seller may be able to do it himself or herself, often at a reduced cost. (When there's already a deal in play, usually the buyer will insist work be done only by a professional, not by the seller.)

Now, when you make an offer with an inspection contingency in it, the sellers may produce the home inspection report and say that they don't want the contingency, because the property has already been inspected and, presumably, has passed (or repairs have been made to defects).

Should you accept the seller's inspection report? You can and it will save you the several hundred bucks for your own inspection. If the house is fairly new and you're savvy about what to look for, accepting could make sense.

On the other hand, how do you know that the seller's inspector did a good job? How do you know that the inspection wasn't done by the sellers' brother-in-law? If the report was done six months earlier, how do you know something hasn't broken since? In short, for such a big investment, why trust someone else's report?

My suggestion is that, with the caveats noted earlier, you insist on your own inspection report and a contingency clause. I can't imagine a serious seller refusing to allow you to have a reinspection.

HOW DO I FIND A GOOD HOME INSPECTOR?

It's important to understand that home inspections are a relatively recent phenomenon. They've only come into vogue within the past ten years as a way to protect buyers (and sellers) against hidden defects in property. As a result, most states do not have laws regulating home inspectors. Indeed, in almost all states, as of this writing, almost anyone can claim to be a home inspector—you, me, or the seller!

This does not mean that competent, qualified inspectors aren't out there. They are. It's just that they are not state licensed and regulated the way real estate agents are.

Thus, my suggestion is that when you look for a home inspector, begin with those people who belong to a trade organization. At least this suggests professionalism on the part of the inspector. There are two major trade organizations.

www.ashi.com

The American Society of Home Inspectors (ASHI) members must pass education and test requirements and must agree to follow a code of ethics. Perhaps more important, the organization has developed "standards of practice" guidelines that cover the home inspection process. Members making inspections are encouraged to follow these guidelines. The standards are thorough and cover virtually every feature of a home. A qualified inspector following the ASHI guidelines should result in your receiving a formidable home inspection.

At the ASHI Web site, you can get much more information about the organization. In addition, it has links to sites in different states operated by members, as well as e-mail addresses and phone numbers of participating members (see Figure 9.1).

www.nahi.org

The National Association of Home Inspectors (NAHI) was established in 1987. It also works to educate and regulate home inspectors. You can

FIGURE 9.1

ASHI home page.

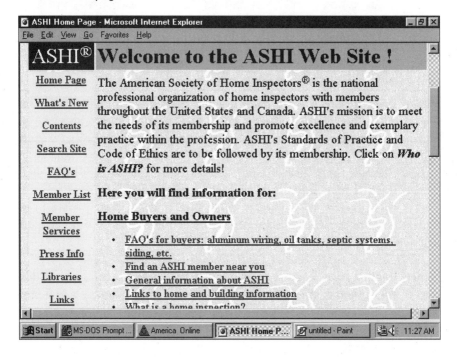

quickly get a list of all its members in your state. NAHI offers education and seminars, as well as a referral service, to those who want to improve their home inspection skills (see Figure 9.2).

In addition to the two national groups mentioned previously, there are also many statewide home inspector trade organizations. The easiest way to locate these is to use a search engine (such as Yahoo!) and search for "home inspector" or "home inspections." You should be given a long list of organizations. You may want to contact one for information more specific to your own state.

How Do I Qualify a Home Inspector?

Once you've gotten a list of four or five potential inspectors in your area, the next thing you should do is to qualify the inspector. Try to determine just how good a job this person will do.

FIGURE 9.2

NAHI home page.

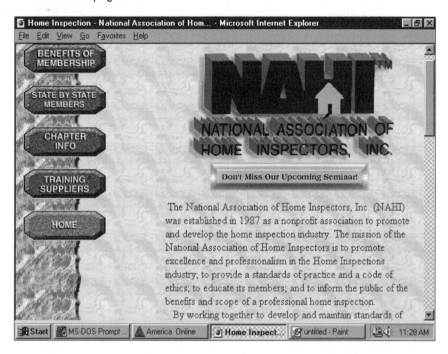

Your potential inspector should have membership in a trade organization, as noted before. But in addition, here are some other ways to check him or her out:

Ask for recommendations The inspector should be able to provide you with half a dozen names, addresses, and phone numbers/e-mail addresses of previous customers. Call or e-mail them. Ask how good a job the inspector did? If it has been at least six months or more since the inspection, ask if something turned up after the people moved into the property that they feel the inspector should have caught. Comments of previous clients can be very revealing.

Ask for credentials It goes without saying that the inspector should be a member of a trade organization, as noted before. But beyond that, what qualifies him or her to inspect property? Does the inspector have a degree in structural engineering? In soils? In some

WARNING

Be just a little bit wary of inspectors recommended by real estate agents. Most agents will, indeed, recommend a highly qualified person. But some agents, to get a quick deal, may simply want an inspector who will give a cursory review of the property and then pass it without much comment. If an agent suggests a home inspector, check out that inspector just as thoroughly as you would anyone else.

other area? Degrees usually, but not always, indicate competence.

Many times former contractors will become home inspectors. Presumably they have some knowledge of construction, but that may be limited to putting up new structures. Just being a contractor doesn't necessarily mean a person knows about or understands potential defects in older homes. Besides, if the person was a general contractor, he or she may not know the specifics of electric or plumbing. On the other hand, a former plumbing contractor may know next to nothing about structural problems. Just being a former contractor does not, of itself, mean the person is qualified to be a home inspector.

I find that some of the best home inspectors were former city or county building inspectors. These people were trained to check out not only new work, but remodeling as well, and many times they were called upon to determine if a home had problems serious enough to warrant condemnation. They usually know what to look for.

SHOULD I ACCOMPANY THE INSPECTOR?

I suspect that people who buy a home on-line tend to want to handle things more or less by remote control. Locating and ordering an inspector can be done entirely at home by using the Internet and the phone.

But, it's a different story when it comes time for the actual examination. It will pay big dividends if you go along with the inspector.

The reason is that although the product of the home inspection is a written report, a great deal more than what's put down in writing can be learned by chatting with the inspector along the way.

For example, I can recall examining a support wall in the hillside backyard of a home I was purchasing. The inspector pointed out exactly where several beams were rotted, and he suggested that replacing those would add years to the life of the wall. The report, however, only stated that the wall showed indications of rot, which might or might not affect its life expectancy. I learned far more from the inspector's oral comments than the written report.

In another case, an inspector pointed out cracks in a slab (a cement ground floor) and suggested that they were probably old and I shouldn't be overly concerned about them. She said that because the house was twenty-five years old and the cracks hadn't become worse in that period of time, it was unlikely they'd grow bigger or become a problem in the future. The report, however, indicated cracks in the slab, which might or might not be significant.

The point here is that you can quickly establish a rapport with the inspector and learn a whole host of things, both good and bad, that might not end up in the written report. Anything the inspector puts in writing, he or she must stand behind. Therefore, in my experience, inspectors tend to couch every statement with disclaimers or conditions.

In short, if you want the real "skinny" on what's wrong with the property, go along with the inspector and ask questions.

DO I NEED SPECIALTY INSPECTIONS?

Sometimes the inspector will indicate that he or she really can't give you a definitive

WARNING
Be wary of calling in contractors in lieu of inspectors. For example, an inspector may want several hundred dollars to give an opinion on how to handle a roofing or structural problem. On the other hand, a roofing or general contractor will gladly come in for free to give you a bid on doing the job. However, the contractor has an automatic conflict of interest— he or she wants the work and may pitch both the problem and the solution one way or another to suit themselves. On the other hand, an independent inspector, presumably, is only there to look out for your interests.

WARNING

If the lender gets wind of the fact that the house needs a new roof, it may insist the work be done before it will fund the mortgage. That's why sometimes savvy buyers will insist on simply a price reduction in the sales agreement without specifying the reason.

answer. For example, the inspector may go into the attic and point out that there are pinpoints of light coming through the roof, indicating that it probably leaks. But, can the roof be fixed, or must it be replaced? The inspector truly may not know and may, instead, suggest you call in a roofing inspector.

Or, there may be indications of water in the basement. It might be summer and the basement could be dry, but the inspector may note watermarks on the walls, indicating standing water in the wet winter months. The inspector found the problem, but what's causing it? You may need to call in a soils engineer to find out.

Specialty inspections can be quite expensive—from $500 to $1000 or more. But, if they help define a problem, and particularly if they suggest a solution, they can be well worth the expense.

WHAT WILL THE INSPECTION COST?

This depends on the area of the country you are in and the going rate for home inspections. Typically, the cost will be anywhere between $225 and $400.

Be aware that although an individual inspector may not be willing to negotiate the price for an inspection, the price varies enormously between inspectors. For a home I recently purchased, I got three bids from inspectors, all of whom I considered qualified. The low bid was $225; the high bid was $350. It all depends on how busy the inspector happens to be and what they feel they can charge for their work. (A high bid does not necessarily indicate a better inspector, nor does a low bid indicate a less qualified one.)

WHO GETS THE INSPECTION REPORT?

This seems rather obvious. You pay for the inspection, so you get the report. However, the seller may insist on a copy of the report as well.

The reason the seller wants a copy, in addition to finding out exactly what the report says, is that in many states sellers are required to disclose any information they have on the property. If an inspection was conducted, even if you paid for it, and then you subsequently don't buy the property, the sellers must disclose that report to any future buyers. If the sellers don't have a copy, they can't disclose it. That's why savvy sellers will write into the sales agreement a sentence stating that they are to receive a copy of the inspection report.

CAN I NEGOTIATE A BETTER PRICE ON THE BASIS OF THE INSPECTION?

That depends, of course, on what the inspection reveals. If the inspector finds nothing wrong with the property, then there's no basis to renegotiate. As is more likely, however, particularly with older homes, if the inspector does find some problem, then renegotiations are in order.

If the problem is minor, then usually the sellers will indicate that they will take care of fixing it. For example, there might be a leaky faucet and a couple of screens missing from windows. More likely than not, the sellers will simply agree out-of-hand to take care of this.

But, it could be more serious. The inspector could find that the heat exchanger in the furnace is damaged. The cost to fix the heat exchanger could be $1200. On the other hand, the cost of a new furnace might be $1800. In a situation like this, the sellers may agree to pay $1200 toward the price of a new furnace. And it might behoove you to come up with the remaining $600. To my

WARNING
In truth, the negotiations can continue right up until the deed is signed and the property changes hands! I've seen deals in which a particularly aggressive buyer or seller has repeatedly refused to fulfill requirements previously agreed to unless and until some further concession is made. Often only the threat of a lawsuit will force this person to continue on as agreed, and even then, it may be reluctantly.

way of thinking, a new furnace is always better than a new heat exchanger.

Or, it could be more serious. The inspector could discover that the roof not only was leaking, but was so old that it could not be repaired. The cost of putting on a new roof might amount to between $10,000 and $15,000, depending on the type.

The sellers might balk at this, saying that they've been living in the house for years and the roof only leaks occasionally. They're perfectly satisfied with the way it is, and if it does leak, they'll continue to patch it.

Now it's time for negotiation. You may want to insist on a reduction in price equivalent to the cost of reroofing as a condition of your purchase—no price reduction, no purchase. Or you may insist the work be done by the seller, to your standards, prior to the purchase as a condition of the sale.

Or it could be extremely serious. The inspection may reveal that the house is over a natural waterway. During the wet seasons, a stream develops and that has severely weakened the foundation. Seventy-five thousand dollars worth of repair work may be necessary to correct the problem.

You may want to pass on a house with such a serious defect. However, I have known people who have negotiated a huge price decrease because of a similar problem and then did much of the work themselves, saving tens of thousands of dollars in the process.

WHEN DO THE NEGOTIATIONS END?

In today's real estate environment, the negotiations don't usually end when the deal is signed. Besides the matter of disclosures (discussed earlier in this chapter), there's also the matter of the inspection. Ten or fifteen days later, when the inspection report is in, if something serious is revealed, negotiations can start up all over again. Remember, in a properly worded inspection contingency clause, you the buyer have the right to back out of the deal without penalty if a problem is uncovered.

A home inspection can be your best protection against getting a problem house. Get a good inspector, go along, and if necessary, renegotiate. You'll end up far more satisfied with the deal you get.

10

CHAPTER

WHAT ABOUT TOXICS IN THE HOUSE?

Ten years ago, or even five, there wouldn't be a chapter in a book such as this on toxics. Homes were just assumed to be environmentally safe. They're where we live and sleep. How could they be anything but safe?

However, in recent years a number of disquieting facts regarding toxic problems in homes have come to light. This is particularly the case with older homes, but it can affect some newer homes as well. The issues involve a whole range of toxic agents that can be located in a typical home—lead, asbestos, radon gas, formaldehyde, and copper, to name only a few. If these agents are present, they could cause serious health problems. The question becomes, how do you know if they're in the home you're considering?

In the last chapter we talked about a home inspection. However, although a home inspector will usually do a careful job of checking for physical damage, most inspectors will not check for toxic agents. Rather, this requires separate testing, usually for each toxic agent suspected.

Should you be concerned about toxics in the home you're buying? There's certainly no reason to panic. However, a reasonable level of concern is appropriate, particularly in older homes.

WARNING

Don't think that just because the home was built after 1978 there's no chance lead paint could have been used. The federal ban actually allowed builders and painters to use up existing supplies of lead-based paint. Hence, a home built in 1978 or 1979 or, conceivably, even later, could still have lead paint in it.

SHOULD I WORRY ABOUT LEAD?

Lead paint often exists in homes built prior to 1978 when lead was banned from paint.

The toxic effects of lead poisoning often do not appear for many months, until the lead in the bloodstream rises to dangerous levels. But, they can cause such problems as hyperactivity, high blood pressure, muscle and joint pain, loss of hearing, and more. The effects are especially devastating to children whose growing bodies can absorb the metal more easily. Also, children are more likely to chew on a windowsill covered with lead paint or to place their hands in their mouths after touching lead paint.

If you are concerned about lead in the home you are considering purchasing, you should have the home tested. The government aids you here. It is now a federal law that the seller must disclose to the buyer any knowledge of lead paint in the home. (Most sellers, however, simply say they have no knowledge of lead paint, which is usually true.) However, the seller is also required to give you a booklet describing the dangers of lead in the home and to allow you ten days to conduct an inspection. If after the inspection you find lead in the home, you can negotiate to have it removed or can gracefully back out of the deal.

Inspections, however, cannot be conducted by laypeople. Normally, they require the efforts of a qualified inspector. The inspector will check for lead paint in the house, on the outside, and on the ground. The inspector will also normally check for lead in the water.

The cost of a home inspection for lead usually runs $300 and up. Because of the cost, few home buyers are usually willing to pay for it. On the other hand, if there is lead paint in the home and the decision is made to have it removed, it can cost tens of thousands of dollars for the removal. Lead paint can be removed only by a qualified technician.

If you are concerned that the home you are buying has a lead problem, you should raise the issue during your inspection period and certainly before the sale is concluded. If there is a problem, you don't want to be stuck with all the costs of remedying it later on. You certainly want the seller to pay his or her fair share (if not the total bill).

To learn more about the problems of lead in the home check the following Web site:

www.epa.gov/iaq/lead.html (see Figure 10.1)

SHOULD I WORRY ABOUT ASBESTOS?

Some people pooh-pooh the problems with asbestos, pointing out that most of us have been living with it in the home without concern for decades. However, there is much evidence to indicate that asbestos can be highly dangerous. Breathing asbestos fibers in high levels can lead to an increased risk of lung cancer and other cancers, such as mesothelioma, and a scarring of the lungs called asbestosis, according to the American Lung Association.

Asbestos can be found in many places in the home. In years past, so-called acoustical, or textured, ceilings often contained asbestos. Insulation, particularly on duct work or hot water pipes, also frequently contained asbestos. In addition, it has been used in roof shingles and in some vinyl flooring. Even the artificial embers used in some fireplaces may contain asbestos.

Again, as with lead, you need a qualified professional to identify asbestos in the home. Such an inspection can cost several hundred dollars. However, there is no help here (at the present time) from the government as there is for lead. If you want an asbestos inspection prior to purchase, you'll need to write it in as a contingency in the sales agreement.

HINT
Most modern homes use copper pipes. However, until the 1990s, lead was used in the solder that held these pipes together. This lead can leach into the water in the pipes. Usually, however, this is only a problem in the first five years or so. After that the solder gets coated with deposits and little lead leaches out.

FIGURE 10.1

EPA/lead home page.

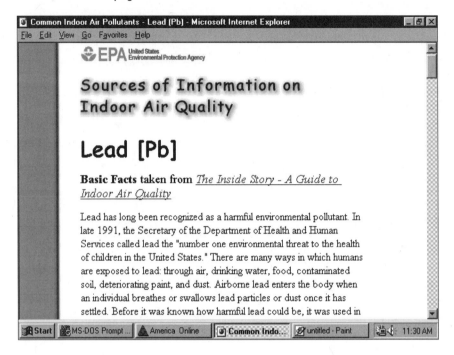

Discovery of asbestos does not necessarily mean it must be removed. Generally speaking, asbestos that stays in place poses little danger. Therefore, encapsulating it or covering it is also sometimes an approved method of dealing with it. However, because any disturbance of asbestos can release fibers into the air, all work on it must be done by qualified professionals—and that can be costly.

For more information on asbestos in the home, check into:

www.epa.gov/iaq/pubs/asbestos.html

SHOULD I BE CONCERNED ABOUT RADON GAS?

Radon is a naturally occurring gas that results from the breakdown of uranium in the soil. The gas drifts upward in the soil and enters homes through basements. When it occurs, it is primarily found in basements and lower floors.

Radon is odorless and colorless and can be detected only by using sophisticated equipment. However, it is far from harmless. The surgeon general has said that radon is the second leading cause of lung cancer in the United States. However, it is not an instant killer. It apparently requires many years of high exposure to radon to produce ill effects.

Radon occurs in dangerous amounts in certain areas of the country. You will probably want to ask your real estate agent and/or county health officer if radon is a concern in your area. If it is, you may want to insist that your new home be inspected for radon prior to purchase. (Often in areas with severe radon contamination, sellers will have already done this and can provide you with documentation showing whether or not the gas is present.)

Home testing kits are available for under $50, but these usually require a month or more to be effective. They are placed in the lowest level of the home and test for radon in the air over time. They are then sent to a laboratory for evaluation and the result sent back to you. Unfortunately, the time frame usually prohibits their use in a purchase situation.

Professionals can test for radon in the home using more expensive equipment in about three days. This, however, costs substantially more. A measurement of four picocuries per liter (4 pCi/L) or more is usually considered a health hazard.

If radon is found, it can almost always be successfully treated. There are several methods, but most involve circulating the air so that contaminants are quickly moved to the outside and aren't allowed to build up under the home.

WARNING
Some people erroneously believe they can remove lead paint by burning or scraping it off. Both processes, however, release it into the air where it can be inhaled. Furthermore, most consumer vacuum cleaners cannot capture lead dust. It is so fine that after being vacuumed, it slips through the container bag and out into the air. For these reasons alone, lead should be removed by a qualified person using special equipment.

Radon mitigation equipment usually costs under $2500, but it can cost more. It can be done by the seller, but if it were me, I'd insist that it be done by a professional, someone listed as qualified for radon mitigation. These listings can be found in the Environmental Protection Agency's (EPA's) National Radon Proficiency Program (see the Web sites hereafter). When properly installed, radon reduction systems can get virtually all of the contaminant out of indoor air.

For more information on radon, the danger it poses, and its reduction, check into the following (see Figure 10.2). The last two offer helpful guides:

www.epa.gov/iaq/radon/index.html

www.epa.gov/iaq/radon/pubs/consguid.html

www.epa.gov/iaq/radon/pubs/hmbyguid.html

FIGURE 10.2

EPA/radon home page.

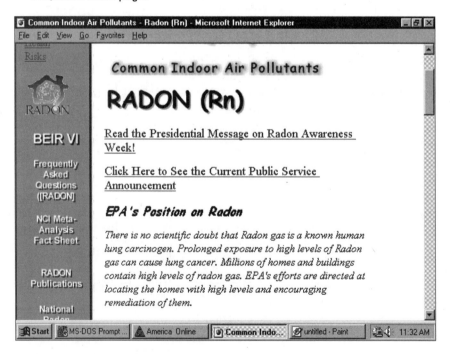

SHOULD I WORRY ABOUT FORMALDEHYDE?

Formaldehyde is a colorless gas that is given off by some building materials. When it is in a strong concentration, it has a pungent odor that can make your eyes water and even cause nausea in some people. In lower concentrations, it may be barely noticeable.

Formaldehyde in the home usually comes from pressed wood and plywood products, although it can also be a by-product of combustion and, as such, can be produced by kerosene and other heaters. It is also found in some paints and glues.

In terms of pressed wood and plywood, there are actually two different types of formaldehyde resin used as glue: phenol-formaldehyde, which produces lower levels of the gas, and urea-formaldehyde, which produces much higher levels. Today most products use the lowest level of formaldehyde-producing odor possible.

Formaldehyde is most likely to be noticed in new homes, particularly those that have plywood or pressed-wood paneling. In older homes, it may come from insulation that was installed as foam in the walls, a common practice in the 1970s. Generally speaking, formaldehyde odors tend to dissipate over time.

When you are purchasing a home, your best clue to a formaldehyde problem is your nose. It's a good idea to conduct an inspection on a house in which all the doors and windows have been closed for some time. That allows any odors to build up and it is more likely they will be detected.

Formaldehyde odors are usually removed by getting rid of the pressed wood, plywood, or other material that is causing the problem. Sometimes painting over the offending item will work; however, that

WARNING
Be wary of a home that has all the windows and doors open (usually protected with screens) every time you inspect the property. It could be that the seller is simply trying to be sure the place is aired out so you never get a chance to smell peculiar odors that could affect your decision to purchase or the price you might offer.

H I N T

If you detect formaldehyde odors in a home, it's something you will want to bring to the seller's attention. You may want to call in a contractor to get an estimate of the cost of replacing the offending material, and reducing your offer by at least that much money.

usually requires painting not only the front surface, but the side and rear surfaces as well, something that simply may not be possible in installed products.

You can get more information on formaldehyde in the home by checking out:

www.epa.gov/iaq/pubs/insidest.html

SHOULD I WORRY ABOUT COPPER IN THE HOME?

Copper in the home usually occurs in the water system. Indeed, copper water systems are considered state-of-the-art, the best you can have, at least when compared with the old galvanized pipe systems. (PVC systems have not yet been approved for potable water in most jurisdictions around the country.)

Problems can occur, however, if copper leaches out of the pipes and gets into the drinking water. Drinking large amounts of copper in water can cause gastrointestinal irritation. It also could have other harmful effects.

Generally speaking, copper in the water is not a problem. In some areas of the country, however, it has become so. These are often called "blue water" areas. The reason is that when copper is dissolved in water, it causes the water to turn a bluish color.

There are numerous chemicals that can cause copper to dissolve, including acids and strong chlorine. There have been cases reported in which the overchlorinating of a water supply has, apparently, resulted in leaching copper out of pipes. It may also be the case that cheap copper pipes (often manufactured in third-world countries), blended with other metals to increase hardness, may also allow some leaching.

Again, check with an agent and the public health officer in your community to see if a problem exists in the area of the home you are considering. Chances are it doesn't. But if it does, it could be very serious and could adversely affect your ability to resell the property. When it occurs, copper in the water often comes from pipes in the delivery system to the house, not from the house itself. Therefore, an owner's ability to correct the situation is limited.

SHOULD I WORRY ABOUT ANY OTHER TOXICS?

There are other chemicals that can cause problems, such as oil contamination of the ground or carbon monoxide coming from a leaking vent in a gas-burning appliance. You should have your home inspector (see the last chapter) check these out for you.

However, there is one last area that I think is worth covering, which few people ever consider: animal odors.

Animal odors are not normally considered toxic. However, they can really spoil your purchase if they turn up in strong concentrations.

The worst is probably cat urine. If cats are allowed to urinate on floors, the odor will set in and it will be almost impossible to get it out. I frequently tell the story of some friends who bought a home, not suspecting any such problem. When they saw the home, the sellers always had the windows and doors open and the place aired out so there were few odors present.

However, the day they moved in happened to be cool and they closed the doors and windows at night. By morning the urine odor was overwhelming. The children were sneezing and coughing and the adults' eyes were running. They had to move out and into a motel.

The story was that the sellers had allowed their cats free rein of the home, and the animals had urinated throughout on the carpeting. It was contaminated in virtually every room.

Regardless of what carpet cleaners may tell you, my personal experience is that cat (or dog for that matter) urine cannot be removed or neutralized. The carpeting, padding, and in some cases, the subflooring must be replaced. (I once had a home in which the urine was in the cement slab,

HINT

If you're buying a home in which the water supply is fed by a well, be absolutely sure you get a report on the quality of the well water. You not only want to watch out for toxic chemicals, but bacteria as well.

which could not be replaced. I treated it with Pine-Sol and other chemicals over a period of several weeks to finally get the odor out.)

All of which is to say be careful about pet odors, particularly from urine, in the home. Whenever I'm serious about a house, I actually get down on all fours and sniff the carpeting and floors in several of the rooms, just to be sure. I'm certain the agent and the sellers think I'm crazy. But, they quickly change their tune if I discover a urine contamination problem.

In this chapter, we've looked at dealing with a number of toxics in the home. As I said at the onset, ten years ago this might not have been considered a problem of consequence. Today it is. If you don't deal with it when you buy, you'll have to deal with it when you resell. And that could cost you really big bucks.

11
CHAPTER

SPECIAL CONCERNS WITH CONDOS AND CO-OPS

Condos and co-ops are often considered the first choice by many buyers who want to pay a lower price (usually), have reduced outside maintenance, and participate in a group lifestyle. Sometimes they are purchased as second homes in vacation areas, but often they are the primary home.

Although condos and co-ops do offer many desirable alternatives, they also present the buyer with some serious pitfalls. In this chapter, we'll look at buying a condo/co-op on-line from both perspectives.

IS BUYING A CONDO/CO-OP ON-LINE DIFFERENT FROM BUYING A SINGLE-FAMILY RESIDENCE?

Not really. However, it can be easier in some ways because, in a group living situation, there are often many similar units and finding comparables for sales comparisons can be much easier. Furthermore, occasionally a larger condo/co-op will have its own Web site and will provide all sorts of valuable information about the facility.

If you need to contact the home owners' association (HOA) and it has a Web site, you'll very quickly find that it's far quicker to get the right information by asking for it over e-mail, than by having to go down to an office and pry it out of a busy secretary.

WHAT ARE THE POSITIVES ABOUT CONDO/CO-OP LIVING?

As noted earlier, when you buy into a shared-ownership property (either condo or co-op), you are actually trading off a portion of your privacy in exchange for a reduced price (usually), guaranteed maintenance, and shared lifestyle. These can be very valuable assets, although some people note that condominium ownership is very much like living in an apartment.

In shared properties, there are often gardeners and workpeople who will tend to any lawn or shrubs in front of your unit. When the outside of the building needs painting, the home owners' association will take care of it. When a new roof needs to go on, usually (but not always) the HOA will do that too.

Also, there may be many get-togethers, including barbecues, birthday parties, and the like. And you may have access to amenities, such as swimming pools, spas, tennis courts, even golf courses in some cases. Usually only home owners are allowed into these areas, so often they are not in the least bit crowded.

If you want a lifestyle that doesn't tie you down to the home, if you want to be able to leave and know that there will be someone nearby who can watch out for your home while you're gone, if you want low maintenance, if you want better locations at lower prices, then a condo/co-op may be perfect for you.

WHAT ARE THE NEGATIVES?

Unfortunately, nothing in life is perfect. Condos/co-ops have their share of problems, and you should be aware of them before you leap in.

Low Selling Prices

The old rule in real estate is that condos/co-ops are usually the last to see price appreciation when times are good, and the first to see price declines when the market takes a nosedive. That's the old rule. The new rule emphasizes, only in some cases.

Condos/co-ops have more recently been built in top-flight areas and, as such, sometimes have better price performance than single-family homes. It depends on *where* they are located.

Today, buy a condo/co-op near the beach, at the lake, in the mountains, downtown—any highly desirable location and the old rule probably doesn't apply. Your condo/co-op investment in prime locations should hold its price right up there with the single-family homes.

Of course, that doesn't apply to condos/co-ops in less-than-prime locations. In the suburbs, don't expect them to hold their values nearly as well.

High Density

Your neighbors are only a thin wall away. In a condo/co-op, you aren't "lord of all you survey." You have to keep the stereo down so as not to bother the other nearby owners; if they don't keep their noise down, it could bother you. Of course, you can always complain to the HOA, which may or may not be able to solve the problem. In this respect, it's much like living in an apartment.

Lack of Control

Although you can usually do pretty much what you want inside your unit, you normally can't change or paint the outside of your building in any significant way. If you don't like the flower arrangement in front of your door, you may have to get the HOA's permission to change it. [This also applies to single-family homes with strict conditions, covenants, and restrictions (CC&Rs)—I recently bought a single-family home where I must get permission to add or cut down a tree in front of my property from the HOA!]

Conflict

Nothing runs as badly, in most cases, as an HOA. I've been to board meetings in which there were actual fistfights between various owners! No matter what needs to be done, there are owners who are for it and those who are against it, and the arguments can last interminably. I once was on the board of an HOA that owned a golf course, and we spent an entire summer trying to decide whether to put a port-a-potty on the course!

Yet, to protect your own interests, you'll find that you want to be on the HOA board yourself. Although at first this seems an innocuous enough task, beware of HOA burnout. This comes after you've been a member of the board for a year or two and found that you can't get done what you want to get done. I've seen owners get so discouraged that they will sell their units, just to be rid of the conflicts that the HOA engenders.

WHAT BASIC PRECAUTIONS SHOULD I TAKE BEFORE I BUY?

There are a number of items to check out before you make your purchase. We'll cover three here: tenants; bylaws; and CC&Rs, dues, and lawsuits.

Check the Ratio of Owners to Tenants

This is a great way to quickly determine how good a condo or co-op may be. In good situations, there are very few tenants. The vast majority of units are occupied by owners. In other words, the place is so good that lots of people want to own property there.

On the other hand, nothing says a bad situation more than having lots of tenants. This means that there are many nonresident owners who are holding the property for rental. This sometimes means they can't sell, so they are renting it out. Also, tenants never seem to take care of a place as well as the owners, and they tend to be noisier. If you're going to buy into a situation with a lot of tenants, be aware that it's much more like moving into an apartment building.

What constitutes good and bad ratios? Generally having tenants as less than 10 percent of the residents indicates a good condo/co-op. When tenants exceed 25 percent of the residents, watch out. There's probably something wrong going on that you just don't see.

Check Out the Bylaws and CC&Rs

Home owners' associations get their authority from the adopted bylaws and recorded conditions, covenants, and restrictions (CC&Rs). You want these rules to be strict, so the HOA can take care of property owners who are too loud, who park their cars in the wrong spot, or who don't pay their dues.

On the other hand, sometimes the rules are so strict that it's not worth living there. One example in point is an HOA that precluded children from using the pool or spa. Not usually a bad idea in an adult community. But, when an owner's grandchildren came over for the day, the HOA kept them out, too. It was a case in which there were too many or too restrictive rules.

My suggestion is that you take the bylaws and CC&Rs to an attorney for evaluation. Usually, it's pretty hard for a layperson to determine whether they're okay or they're a problem.

Check Out the Monthly Dues

These can be quite high. I recently backed out of the purchase of a condominium unit in a very desirable location because the dues were over $300 a month. My feeling was that this was so high that I'd have difficulty later on reselling.

Also, check out the history of the dues. Sometimes they are kept artificially low when the unit is first built to attract first-time buyers. However, because they are so low, not enough money is put into reserve funds so that years later, when a building needs to be repainted or a new roof put on, there's no money available to do it. At that time, a loan is usually obtained and the dues sharply increased to cover the loan payments.

Watch out for condos/co-ops in which there have been sharp dues increases in the past; it indicates a poorly run organization. And, sharp increases in the past can indicate that sharp increases will occur in the future.

Check Out Any Lawsuits

It seems that home owners are forever suing the HOA. An owner will get mad because he or she has been rebuffed by the board of directors and a lawsuit follows. This would be comic if it weren't so serious. A lawsuit against the HOA can mean that lenders won't offer financing on any of the units, which means that you wouldn't be able to easily resell later on.

When buying into a condo or co-op, be sure to ask if there are any pending lawsuits against the HOA. If there are, you will want to have a lawyer analyze them to see if they present a problem. Losing a lawsuit may mean that each owner could be assessed to pay off the loss! You will want to seriously reconsider buying into a condo/co-op that has an active lawsuit against it.

Also, check for a history of lawsuits. If there have been many filed, it suggests a bad organization, one that you may not want to join.

We've covered many of the pros and cons of condos and co-ops. However, we haven't yet defined them. I've assumed that most people know what they are. However, if you've got any lingering doubts, here's a technical explanation.

WHAT IS A CONDO?

As most buyers know, a *condominium* is a kind of shared ownership. Typically, you end up separately owning the inside of the unit while sharing with the other owners all the grounds, walkways, recreational facilities— in short, everything outside. Another way to look at it is as if you were renting an apartment and then decided to buy your rental unit. (Indeed, some condos are converted apartment houses.)

It's sometimes useful to know that there are actually at least two separate kinds of condominium-type ownership. The first is the one with which most people are familiar—you could be on the fifth floor of a building and you own only that airspace that your unit occupies.

The second is sometimes called a townhouse (technically known as a planned-unit development, or PUD). Here, units are not arranged on top of each other; rather, each unit has its own ground space below and airspace above. You actually own the ground beneath your townhouse. Because townhomes usually have a lower density of ownership than condos, they tend to be more highly desired, to command a higher price initially and on resale, and to be easier to sell.

WHAT IS A CO-OP?

On the other hand, a *co-op* is a cooperatively owned property. This is a different sort of ownership in that you, as an individual, don't actually own any separate airspace or ground. Rather, you own a share of stock in a company that owns the entire property. Although you have the exclusive right to use a particular unit, you don't actually own it in the sense of being able to sell it directly. To sell your unit, you must sell your share in the company.

Co-ops are found primarily on the East Coast, mostly in New York. They are often in choice locations and are considered highly desirable properties.

Generally speaking, you should buy a condo/co-op only if you are fully aware of the different type of lifestyle they offer, as well as their pros and cons. It is usually a mistake to buy into a condo, for example, only because it is cheaper than buying into a single-family home in the same area. If you buy a condo/co-op thinking it is only a less expensive form of a single-family house, you're making a mistake and you could regret it all the days that you live there.

If you're not sure, I suggest that you try living in a shared-lifestyle environment for a while. As noted earlier, most facilities offer some units for rent. Rent for six months and try it out. You may find that you love it and will want to buy your very rental unit! Or you could hate it and want to move out the first week, which will be a lot easier to do if you rent than if you buy without first checking it out.

12 CHAPTER

WHEN BUYING FROM A BUILDER

There's nothing like a brand new home. The cabinets are all clean, never before used. The floor is spotless. There are no chips in the sink or tub. The carpeting doesn't have wear marks in the heavily trafficked areas. In short, it's yours to break in as you like; you're not getting someone else's hand-me-down.

This is one of the big reasons that many people look at new homes. Other reasons include location and price. Builders usually put up homes at the outskirts of town where there's room to build; that often (but not always) results in prices that are lower than for existing resales.

WHAT TYPE OF HOME SHOULD I LOOK FOR?

Builders basically offer four types of new homes: condos, townhouses, subdivision houses, and custom-built homes. In some areas they are all mixed together in huge, planned communities. In other cases, there is simply one type alone.

Many people prefer the planned communities for the additional amenities they may offer, such as green belts and walking and bike-riding trails. On the other hand, homes in such areas often cost a bit more.

As most people who have shopped for homes know, except in the case of custom homes, you can normally see the type of home the builder is

HINT

Sometimes appreciation can be fastest in new homes. If a tract of new properties is well located, as soon as it sells out, continuing demand for homes in the area can quickly drive up the price of resales. On the other hand, if the location is poor, the homes may not sell out and it may be difficult to resell. Remember, location is the most important factor.

putting up by looking at models. Usually a builder will put up a sample of each type being constructed on a street near the entrance of the tract or at the entrance to the condo/townhouse area. You are free to wander through these models to see if any attracts your fancy. Usually you will be given a brochure telling the price and features that come with the property. The agent at the model homes can often discuss financing.

HOW DO I FIND NEW HOMES?

The Internet does provide some help here, but as of this writing, not enough. There are services that list new homes, including price, size, location, features, and other amenities by metropolitan area, by state, and by local city. Unfortunately, these services often only include homes in particular states. The National Association of Home Builders (NAHB) also has a Web site with much useful information about builders. Check these Web sites out:

National Association of Home Builders—www.nahb.com This Web site includes information on how to choose a builder, gives important statistics on new home sales, as well as a great deal of other information to help present an overview of new home construction (see Figure 12.1).

CPS New Homes Navigator—www.cpsusa.com/1st/navig.htm This Web site covers some western and eastern states. It offers prices, sales office numbers, builders' names, descriptions of homes, and more.

New Homes Direct—www.newhomesdirect.com This Web site covers homes in some southern states, with indications of branching out to the West and Midwest.

FIGURE 12.1

NAHB Web site.

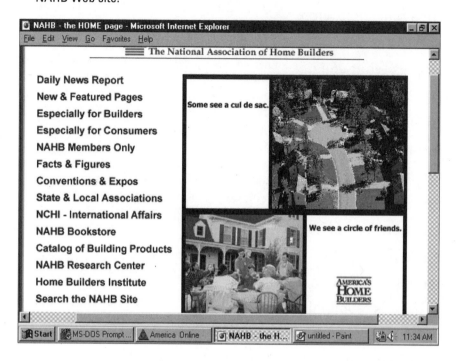

New Homes Quest—www.nhq.com   This Web site covers California, Arizona, and Nevada, as of this writing. It includes a map showing how to locate homes, and it details many of the features offered in the properties.

You'll also probably want to check out new Web sites for finding homes on search engines such as Yahoo!. Try the keywords "new homes for sale."

Many builders also put up their own Web sites. When you check these out, however, pay particular attention to location. You may be in Los Angeles and find just the new home you want at just the right price, only to discover that the builder has homes only in Albuquerque.

In addition to checking out Web sites, look in the local newspaper for ads. Typically, the Saturday or Sunday editions will have a special section on new homes (or at least on real estate in general, including new homes). In many papers there will be a map showing the location of all the new

WARNING

Be aware that what you see is not always what you get with model homes. Obviously, most furnishings are not included, but carpeting, tile and countertops, sinks, appliances, even faucets may all be upgrades, available only at additional cost. What I find particularly deceptive is if there are mirrors on walls or doors that are not included in the base price, because these tend to make rooms appear much larger.

home tracts in the area. Keep in mind, however, that this may not show custom homes.

Also, you can check with your local home builders association. It will have a list of builders who are constructing homes in your area. It can also guide you to custom builders. Also, check with real estate agents; often, they have lists of builders with whom they've successfully dealt. Again, this is particularly helpful for finding good custom builders.

Finally, most areas have new home shows once or twice a year. Builders are often represented here, and it's a good opportunity to talk with them.

HOW DO I CHECK OUT THE NEW HOUSE?

All of the same questions should be asked as when you're checking out any home that you are considering purchasing. (See Chapters 3 and 4.)

In addition, when looking at a new home, be sure to check out the quality of the construction. Look at the cabinets and the carpets. Do you want to upgrade? How much will it cost?

How well done is the trim, the little pieces of molding at the edges of everything? Does the paint look good? Or does it look "weak," as if it's barely on the walls? Good paint looks good. Bad paint looks bad, even when new.

Is the home energy efficient? This is a big concern today with the high price of heating and cooling. At a minimum, the house should be insulated top, bottom, and sides. Double-pane windows are a plus, as is an energy-efficient roof. (Just having a lighter, rather than darker, roof can save a lot on air conditioning in the summer months.) Are the air conditioner, furnace, and water heater all high–energy efficient? It costs more to put this into a property when built, but it saves on utility bills every month you live there.

Finally, don't just shop price. Just because one home costs more than another does not necessarily mean that it is better built.

HOW DO I CHECK OUT THE BUILDER?

When you buy a new home, you're actually buying the reputation of a builder. You want to buy a home from a reputable builder, because it's your assurance that the house was well constructed and won't develop problems down the line.

Probably the best way to learn about a builder's work is to check out homes that he or she has previously built. This is usually quite simple. The builder will normally tell you the location of previous tracts of homes (or, in the case of custom builders, provide you with a list of previous homes constructed). Then, all you need to do is go to those earlier homes and talk to the owners.

Take the time to leave your computer and walk the streets. You should find many owners out working on lawns or gardens. Introduce yourself, explain that you're interested in buying a new home by the same builder as theirs, and ask them if they like the house they bought and have any comments? Usually they will, particularly if they liked or hated the builder.

When you get these comments, be sure to listen to them with a grain of salt. Some people may complain about trivial things: a window screen was torn, and it took a week to get someone out to fix it. The paint on one wall wasn't the agreed-upon color.

Sometimes, however, the complaints are more serious: the home's design is simply bad. The sewers don't work properly, it's been six months, and still no one has come out to fix them. The roof leaks!

Talk to as many people as you can. Don't rely on the comments, good or bad, from just one person. The more people you talk to, the better an understanding of the quality of the builder you're likely to get. Also, be sure to ask the magic question, "Would you buy a home again from this builder?"

You'll also want to ask or e-mail the builder, or his or her representative, some important questions, including the following:

Questions to Ask the Builder

1. How long have you been in business? _____ years.
   (You don't want to be the first customer.)

2. What arrangements have been made for customer service after the sale? _____
   (You want an established, quick, and easy procedure for getting your questions answered and your complaints remedied.)

3. What if something goes wrong with the water heater or the furnace/air conditioner? Is the builder responsible for this? Or do you now have to find and argue with a sub-contractor? _____
   (It's far easier to have one person to contact for everything.)

4. Does the builder belong to a professional trade organization?
   Yes ☐   No ☐
   (Good builders generally do.)

WHAT IS THE INVESTMENT POTENTIAL OF THE NEW HOME?

Is the property likely to appreciate? Will it stay the same in price? Or, will it actually decrease in value?

Part of this is the condition of the overall housing market. But as noted earlier, a large part is also the quality of the home and its location. I can recall some tract homes in Phoenix a few years ago where the resales were selling for substantially less than the new homes, even when comparing identical models of resale and new! The reason was that the builder was able to offer virtually nothing down, low-interest financing, which resellers couldn't match. And buyers simply weren't attracted to the tract, except for price and terms. The houses were traps. You could only get in—you couldn't get out!

As noted, the investment performance of a home down the line also depends, of course, on the real estate market. In a stable market (i.e., no rapid price appreciation or depreciation), there are usually more new homes than buyers, and builders are anxious to sell them off. There are numerous ads in papers, and there are even signs placed along roadways directing potential buyers to model homes. In this type of market, the salespeople typically will bend over backward to get you to commit, sometimes even offering freebies (such as TV sets, furniture, or trips). Just remember, you're a buyer in a seller's market. Shop around to get the very best deal.

On the other hand, sometimes the market is very hot. Everything is selling quickly. In this case, you may have trouble getting a salesperson to e-mail you back. I've seen cases in which, to get a new house, prospective buyers had to camp outside the sales office for days in advance of the properties being put on the market! You just have to do what is required by market conditions.

Generally speaking, in any market, there is one rule of thumb that can help you make a better purchase decision. It is usually better to buy the middle-sized home in a tract. The reason is it will probably appreciate the fastest. The smallest and largest homes could be too small or too big for most buyers, and they could end up being white elephants when it comes time to resell.

WHAT ARE THE TRAPS TO WATCH OUT FOR?

There are a number of pitfalls that you could tumble into, if you're not careful, when buying a new home. We'll cover several here.

What If the House Isn't Completed?

In many cases, particularly today, all you get to see is the model home. You are told that your home will be very similar (not a duplicate), built on the lot of your choice. (You'll have to pay extra for choice lots.)

The trouble here is that you won't really know what your house is going to be like until it's built. You won't get a feeling for the neighborhood. And a lot of items in the new house may be different from the model home.

Therefore, if at all possible, my suggestion is to always buy a completed home. Some builders do put up homes before they are sold.

What About Delays?

This follows the previous question. Normally, a builder will ask for only a nominal, refundable deposit on an unbuilt home, perhaps under $1000. It's just to hold your place in line, so to speak.

But, because of the lack of commitment on the builder's part, you could wait longer than you anticipated for the home to be built. There could be a labor strike. Building materials could be hard to come by. The builder could simply be inefficient or incompetent. There could be a problem with local building department approval. In short, any of hundreds of different things could happen before your home gets built. My own rule of thumb is to take the amount of time the builder estimates it will take to finish your home and add 50 percent. You probably won't be too far off.

What About Extras?

Unlike with resales, it seems that everything is extra with a new home. We've already mentioned upgrades you may want in such areas as countertops, appliances, and floor coverings.

But there's much more. What about fencing around the house? What about rear and side landscaping? (Front landscaping, because it helps sell the properties, is usually included, but not always.) What about decks and overhangs? What about patios, pools, and spas? These all are often extras you have to add in when you buy new.

Some extras can be very expensive. Sometimes, air conditioning is an extra. Yet, with the climate changing and more hot, muggy weather apparently in store for much of the country, air conditioning is rapidly becoming a necessity.

Sometimes, even the lot location can be extra. The "standard" lot may be in the center of the worst street in the tract. Every other lot has a premium, much higher for views and bigger sizes. With a resale, the premium is built into the price. With a new home, it's often an extra.

List of Possible Extras*

1. Larger or view lot
2. Any changes in the basic construction plan
3. Fences
4. Landscaped yard
5. Upgrade of roof
6. Upgrade of exterior walls
7. Upgrade of carpet or tile
8. Air conditioning (now standard on many homes)
9. Additional mirrors or windows
10. Upgrade of insulation

---

* List from Robert Irwin, *Tips and Traps When Buying a Home, 2nd Edition* (McGraw-Hill, New York, 1997).

11. Upgrade of appliances (e.g., stove, oven, dishwasher, etc.)
12. Upgrade of plumbing fixtures (toilets, sinks, tubs)
13. Larger water heater

WHAT IS THE BUILDER'S WARRANTY?

All builders normally warrant the homes they build. In some states builders are required to warrant the homes against major failure for up to ten years, although one year may be more common for workmanship and materials. Check with the state contractor's licensing board or the building division in your state.

Be sure the warranty you get with the new home is in writing. A verbal warranty, as the old saying goes, isn't worth the paper it's written on.

Some builders carry back their own warranties. In other words, if something goes wrong, the builder himself or herself will be responsible for fixing it. Other builders buy a warranty policy from an insurance company, and the insurance company is responsible for curing defects that appear later on. It's hard to say which is better; it all depends on what's warranted and the quality of the builder or the insurer. Insurers often maintain their own Web sites with useful information and contact numbers. The builder should be able to supply you with their screen address.

Before you make your purchase, you should ask to see a copy of the warranty policy. Take a little time to read it. It will specify what's covered. Be sure that you see that things such as leaking roofs, plugged drains (other than something you do your-

WARNING
Some builders will pooh-pooh an emergency number. They'll point out that, "It's a brand new house . . . what could happen?" The answer, of course, is that something is far more likely to happen in a new house than an existing one in which all the systems have been successfully in service for years. (I'll never forget the time a friend bought a new home and when the water was turned on, it gushed out of the overhead light fixture in the kitchen ceiling! The plumbers had somehow connected water pipes to electrical pipes. That was a real emergency! They do happen.)

self), slipping soil, and such items are fully covered. You don't want a policy that only covers you if a purple elephant runs into your home.

As part of their warranty program, most builders also include a couple of service visits. These are to check and correct for problems with trim, paint, and so on. Ideally, you'll want the check to occur within about a month after you move in (and find out what's really wrong with the place!) and perhaps six months to a year later when hidden problems may surface.

Finally, ask the builder what happens if there's an emergency? What if a water pipe bursts in the wall and water is streaming across your living room? Do you have an emergency number to call? Can someone come out right away? You need to find this out before you buy and the emergency happens.

13
CHAPTER

DEALING WITH
THE CLOSING

Eventually, all the problems will get resolved, and you'll be ready to close the deal. This is when you'll sign the various mortgage documents, the sellers will sign the deed, and the property will actually change hands. It's really just that simple, although in actual practice it can become far more complicated.

Even though you may have found your home on-line and obtained your mortgage over the Internet, chances are that almost certainly you'll have to show up at an escrow or attorney's office for the closing. It's the one part of the transaction that normally must be done in person, at least as of this time.

In this chapter, we'll look at what you can expect, what you need to bring, and how to make it as painless as possible.

WHAT SHOULD I BRING TO THE CLOSING?

The old saw is that the only really essential thing is your checkbook. However, if you've obtained your mortgage on-line and haven't yet presented the required documentation, check with your lender. You may need to bring a whole raft of items, from W-2 and 1040 forms to paycheck stubs, bank and employer verifications.

WHAT ARE THE CLOSING COSTS?

You will have closing costs. Sometimes, these can be big. As we saw in Chapter 8, there are going to be lender's fees, which can amount to thousands of dollars. The escrow service probably will also charge its own fees, which can be costly. Here's a list of typical closing fees, all of which normally will need to be paid in cash at closing. (Note: Not all fees will be charged at all closings):

HINT

Always call the agent, the lender, and the escrow officer (or the attorney handling the escrow) in advance to find out exactly what you need to bring. If some vital document is missing, the escrow won't be able to close until you go back and get it.

Account setup fee
ALTA title insurance fee
Attorney document preparation fee
Attorney fees
Document preparation fee
Escrow document preparation fee
Escrow fee
Home owner's warranty package
Home owner's insurance
Impound collection setup fee
Impound setup/service fee
Insurance proration
Interest proration
IRS filing fee
Loan fee
Mortgage assumption fee
Policy of fire insurance
Recording encumbrance (or release of)
Recording fees for deed
Recording affidavit of value
Recording assumption
Tax service contract
Taxes proration
Title insurance fee

Let's consider some of the more common fees in detail.

Account Setup Fee

This is a relatively new garbage fee. The lender charges you to set up the payback account—the little payment book or monthly invoices you'll get when you pay. I find this charge particularly insulting.

ALTA Title Insurance

Lenders will often insist that you obtain additional insurance called an American Land Title Association (ALTA) policy. It gives the lender additional assurances including, often, an inspection of the property. If the lender requires it, you'll have to pay it.

Assumption Fee

If you're assuming an existing mortgage, you have this to pay. It's typically in the $100 to $300 range. Remember, however, that most mortgages are not assumable, so you probably won't have (or shouldn't have) this charge.

Attorney Fee

HINT
You may not have to pay the escrow fee. Who pays (buyers or sellers) is usually determined by custom in the particular area. Sometimes, it is customary to split these costs with the seller. Check with the escrow officer or your agent. It may be customary for the seller to pay these charges!

If you have your own attorney, which is probably a good idea, you will have to pay this fee. It is typically $500 to $1000 for handling an entire transaction.

However, there may also be a fee for the lender's attorney, for checking over the mortgage documents and the transaction. Again, it's another garbage fee. Unless the deal is unusual in some way, the lender should have attorneys on staff to check documents, not charge you extra for them.

Document Preparation Fee

This is paid to the lender and/or the escrow company for preparing the loan documents. It can amount to $300 or more. To my thinking, because

HINT

As with escrow charges, you may not have to pay the title insurance fee. Who pays (buyers or sellers) is usually determined by custom in the particular area. Sometimes, it is customary to split these costs with the seller. Check with the escrow officer or your agent. It may be customary for the seller to pay these charges.

the lender is making the loan anyway and because it only takes a few taps on a computer keyboard to spit out the documents, it's a garbage fee. However, you may have to pay it to get the financing you want.

Escrow Fee

The company handling the escrow will have it's own charge. The cost usually varies according to the price of the house. A minimum of $250 to $300 is often the case, with the price going much higher, depending on the price of the property.

Home Warranty Package

It typically costs $250 and upward annually, depending on the quality of coverage. *Usually the seller will pay for this,* but not always. A home warranty package protects you if something goes wrong with any of the systems of the property, such as the water heater or garbage disposal. Typically, there's a deductible of $35 to $50 per occurrence, which you pay, and the insurance company picks up the tab for the rest.

Impound Account

If your mortgage is for more than 80 percent of the value of the property, you will be required by the lender to pay one-twelfth of your taxes and insurance each month. *Impound* simply means the holding of tax and insurance money for you (and then paying it out appropriately). Recent legislation has required lenders to be more scrupulous as to how they handle impound accounts and to only demand a minimum amount of money, usually no more than a month or two, for the account at closing.

Many lenders, however, will charge you for setting up this account. This is a separate setup fee.

Insurance Fees

You will want, and the lender will require you, to carry fire and possibly home owner's insurance (the latter giving you much broader coverage). This insures you and the lender in case of fire and other disasters. The cost will vary, depending on the value of the house and the perceived risk by the insurer. Typically, it will cost anywhere from $200 to $1000 a year. You will be required to pay at least one year's insurance in advance. Most policies, however, are written for three-year periods and automatically renew.

Loan Fee

Many lenders will charge a loan fee. It can be in addition to points, for example, two points plus $300. The $300 is the loan fee and usually goes to cover such work as preparing documents and funding the money. Again, this is a garbage fee that most lenders charge today. To get the mortgage, you'll probably simply have to pay it.

WARNING

It's come to light recently that the government has been less than stringent in enforcing RESPA. Although most lenders have been quite strict about providing estimated costs prior to closing, some have taken to grossly underestimating these costs or failing to include all costs in the estimate. Upon closing, many buyers have found that they have far more costs than the original estimate sheet showed. If that's the case, protest loudly. Threaten to take the lender to the FTC (address follows). If there's really a problem and you protest loudly, even at closing, chances are a lender will make an effort to correct the situation. Most lenders simply don't want the bad publicity.

Points

We've already discussed this in Chapter 8. You'll recall that a point is equal to 1 percent of the mortgage. If the mortgage is for $100,000, two points is equal to $2000. You should know well in advance the number of points you'll have to pay. Typically, the mortgage amount that gets funded is minus the points, which you must make up in cash.

Recording Fees

This is the charge by the escrow company for recording documents. The typical cost to record a document is from $7 to $25 per document. This is a true fee and you should expect to pay it.

Tax Prorations

The escrow company prorates your share of the year's taxes. Taxes are usually paid twice annually. Depending on when you buy, the taxes may yet have to be paid on the next installment, or may have already been paid. The escrow company determines whether you owe the sellers money, or they owe it back to you. Usually, you'll never have to pay more than six months worth of taxes.

Tax Service Contract

If you don't have a tax impound account, this contract hires a company to watch your property's tax records. If you fail to pay them, a report is sent to the lender who then pays the taxes, adds the amount onto your mortgage and, often, begins foreclosure. The fee is usually around $25 to $50.

Title Insurance

You need title insurance to protect your claim to the property. Also, no lender will offer a mortgage without title insurance. The cost of title insurance varies according to the price of the property. It might cost you anywhere from $300 on up. Keep in mind that there are lots of title insurance companies. Because for practical purposes one title company is as good as another, it pays to shop fees.

CAN'T I PROTEST THE GARBAGE FEES?

As we've seen, much of what you're charged is, in reality, nothing more than garbage fees. If you wait until escrow is closing to complain about them, it's too late. The lender and escrow company normally won't change anything at this point, and your leverage—to find a different lender or escrow company—is gone. The seller usually won't be interested in holding up the sale while you spend another several weeks searching around.

Therefore, you need to protest fees that you feel are just plain garbage and unjustified when you first find out about them. That's usually at the time you apply for financing.

READ YOUR ESTIMATES OF CLOSING COSTS CAREFULLY

The Real Estate Settlement Procedures Act (RESPA) specifies that a lender must give you a good-faith estimate of what your costs for the loan and, in effect, the transaction (including escrow charges) will be within three days of your submitting a mortgage application. This merely, however, states most (not all) costs.

Read the estimate very carefully. Look for hidden garbage costs. The real advantage of having a good-faith estimate early from a lender is that if the costs are too high, you have time to shop for a loan elsewhere.

Also, ask your real estate agent for an estimate of your closing costs. A good agent can put together a highly accurate estimate even before you make your offer.

You can contact the FTC for problems (see Figure 13.1):

HINT

Sometimes, a way to make a "full-price" offer without actually offering full price is to ask the seller to pay a certain amount, say $5000, in "nonrecurring closing costs." This refers to fees and escrow charges, but does not include interest or similar costs. The seller gives back the money in escrow where it is used to pay for your closing costs. It can sometimes work with a seller who is determined to get his or her price, but is willing to negotiate on terms.

FIGURE 13.1

FTC home page.

Federal Trade Commission
Division of Credit Practices
Consumer Response Center
Room 130
6th Street and Pennsylvania Ave., N.W.
Washington, D.C. 20580
(202) 382-4357 (FTC-HELP)
www.ftc.gov

CAN I NEGOTIATE FEES WITH THE SELLER?

Indeed you can, but it must be part of the overall negotiations for the purchase of the home. When you make your offer, there's nothing to prevent you from writing a clause into your contract specifying that the seller will pay all or a portion of your closing costs. Of course, the seller may not be eager to do this.

14

CHAPTER

FAQS WHEN BUYING A HOME ON-LINE

If you've read through this book, by now you should have an excellent idea of how to buy a home on-line. You should know where to find listings, how to approach agents and sellers, how to make a successful offer, get a mortgage, inspect the property, and handle the closing—in short, the entire on-line purchase process.

However, it may be comforting to have a separate chapter on just the various traps you're likely to run into, as well as the many tips to use to your advantage. That's what this chapter will accomplish. Here's a list of FAQs (frequently asked questions) to help you be sure you're on track when buying on-line.

1. Should I search only a single Web site?

Remember, there are dozens, thousands out there. Take the time to check out many of them. The vast majority of the resales in the country are now listed electronically. You stand an excellent chance of finding the right house for you by going on-line, perhaps better than hunting for it the old-fashioned way. Check Chapter 2.

2. Should I search for properties listed by sellers?

The Internet provides a wonderful opportunity for FSBOs to publicize their property. You'll find all sorts of homes listed by owners, often at

155

steep discounts. This area is bound to grow increasingly as sellers opt to save money on commissions and pass some of those savings onto you. Check Chapter 2.

3. Should I buy location first?

Buy in a location close to work, to schools, to shopping, to hospitals and doctors, even to recreational facilities, and no matter what your needs or desires, you'll find them quickly and easily met. Which is to say you'll enjoy living there. Buy all this, but even more, buy in a desirable area that has seen and is likely to continue to see rapid price appreciation. Check Chapter 3.

4. Should I look only at home Web sites, not at community Web sites?

Schools, cultural activities, crime, industries and businesses, and shopping all make up a community. If the stats are good, you'll want to live there—and so will others, making reselling later on far quicker and more profitable. If you don't want to live in the community, why would you buy there, even if the particular house you've found seems terrific? Check Chapter 3.

5. Should I check commute times instead of mileage?

Remember, commuting distance is usually measured in time, not miles. It really doesn't matter how far away your home is from work; what matters is how long it takes to get there. Good access to freeways, rapid transit, even airports can be more important than physical proximity. Check Chapter 3.

6. When using a location wizard, should I beware of asking for a smaller house because it's easier to maintain?

True, but it may not be easier to resell. And, when you have company or need more space, you'll find it extremely expensive to add on. In general (not always, certainly), buying a bit bigger than you think you need works out best. Check Chapter 3.

7. Should I ask for at least three bedrooms, two baths?

You'll find that a home with at least three bedrooms is always easier to sell. Besides, even if there are only two or even one of you, you'll quickly fill up the extra room. It won't go to waste. At least two baths is a necessity, not an option. If you don't believe it, just happen to be in a one-bathroom house when two people need to use it. Check Chapter 3.

8. What if I fall in love with the on-line photo?

A picture is worth a thousand words, certainly. But, pictures can't tell the entire story. Look at the details in the listings. Many Web sites feature big images of homes shot to their best advantage. But information as to lot and building size, location, layout, and much more is just as, if not more, important. By the way, more pictures will help. A site that can provide you with half a dozen shots of the home will help you get a much better feeling for the property and neighborhood than just one. However, the details are still important. Check Chapter 3.

9. Do I really need to see the property?

Remember, all real estate is unique. Every property is different from every other, from its location on the street to its layout and design to how it's decorated. You can't learn that on-line. Yes, you can narrow your search down to one or two homes. But then, it's obligatory that you visit them. Check Chapter 4.

10. Should I rely on my first impression?

Curb appeal is vital to the salability of a home. If the house doesn't have it, you won't like it when you drive up, and neither will someone else when it's time to resell. Of course, curb appeal can be improved, in some cases, by changing the front landscaping. But many things, such as the way the house fronts the street, cannot be easily changed. If you just don't like the look of the place when you drive up, listen to your feelings. Check Chapter 4.

11. Should I walk the neighborhood before I buy?

It's a big mistake not to. By walking the neighborhood, you can check out the condition of neighboring homes, the street, the noisiness of the neighborhood, graffiti on the walls, and other detractions. You might miss lots of this simply by looking only on-line. And if you're uncomfortable walking around the neighborhood before you buy, just how comfortable will you be once you're living there?! Check out Chapter 4.

12. Should I look up and down when I tour the home?

Carpets and ceilings are important. They can tell you the condition of property faster than almost anything else. They are also some of the most expensive items to refurbish. Check Chapter 4.

13. Should I try to explain away the home's design?

Some homes flow nicely and others have an awkward layout. But sometimes the price is right and you begin saying to yourself that you can handle having the fireplace in the hallway and the bathroom leading out of the kitchen. The trouble is, although you might save money once when you buy, you'll have to live in the house every day. And, every day living in a layout/design that you don't like and that doesn't work for you can be torture. Remember, there are always other homes. Check out Chapter 4.

14. Should I find my agent on-line?

An agent who lists property electronically is going to be savvy about a lot of other things on the Internet, such as financing, and should be of help to you in many ways. Why not find and qualify your agent on-line? Of course, you can reserve final judgment until you actually meet the person, but communication by e-mail and then phone can really establish rapport. Check out Chapter 5.

15. Is it all right to work with lots of on-line agents?

Although it is a good idea to talk to many agents when you're narrowing your search, once you've found an area you like, it's a better idea to find a really good agent and work exclusively with him or her—at least until you find a reason to change. That way, when you finally do locate the house you want, you'll have an agent ready to go with whom you're comfortable. Check into Chapter 5.

16. When finding an agent with whom to work, should I go with my feelings?

Yes, if you're psychic. If not, qualify the agent thoroughly, asking how long they've been in the business, are they active, and can they give you references you can check out. Check into Chapter 5.

17. Should I keep the agent guessing?

If you're just checking a Web site and don't want to be bothered by an agent, then there's no need to pass along any information about yourself. But, if you're working with one agent in particular, then you need to tell the agent enough to let them do their job. That includes what you really want and how much you can really afford. Check out Chapter 5.

18. Does the agent you talk with work for you?

Maybe, but probably not. You want to find a buyer's agent, one who is in your corner, not the seller's. Check Chapter 5.

19. How much do I tell the seller?

Unlike an agent, the seller is never on your side. Any information about how much you're willing or able to pay, or whether you're in love with the property, may give the seller ammunition to keep the price up. Mum's the word, here. Check Chapter 5.

20. Is it a mistake to shy away from on-line FSBO sellers?

There are bargains to be had here. The Internet is often the FSBOs biggest means of publicizing a home for sale; if you don't approach by-owner sellers, you may not ever find them. Besides, if you're uncomfortable handling the transaction by yourself, don't worry about it. After you find the property, call in an agent, for half a commission (usually paid by the seller), to handle the details and the paperwork. Check Chapter 5.

21. Should I make my offer only on-line?

You can make a tentative offer on-line. But once you want to nail things down, get confirmation by fax and by mail. Until you have an actual signed and written contract in your hand, you probably don't have a deal. Check into Chapter 6.

22. Should I get an attorney's help?

Many people believe that attorneys are too expensive and only muck up the water in real estate deals. Not so. Most real estate attorneys are incredibly cheap when compared with what lawyers charge for other services. And, they can save you a great deal of hassle later on by correctly drawing documents at the onset (as well as checking out the legal parts of the deal). Check into Chapter 6.

23. How big a deposit should I offer?

You need to offer enough to show you are in earnest. But, that doesn't have to be half the down payment. Remember, whatever you offer as a deposit is at risk. If things go wrong, there is always the chance you could lose the money. See Chapter 6.

24. *Should I always make a lowball offer first?*

A lowball offer tests the waters. An eager seller might just accept it. But, know your market. In a hot market, while you're playing games with a lowball offer, another buyer may come in with a more realistic offer and steal the property away from you. Check out Chapter 6.

25. *Should I look first for a mortgage on-line?*

It's a good idea. You'll find the biggest bargains there. Often, the same mortgage is offered for fewer points or a lower interest rate on-line than in the physical marketplace. But be sure you know what you want and understand the mortgage market. No one's going to hold you by the hand while you search for a mortgage on-line. Check Chapter 7.

26. *Should I get preapproved?*

A commitment from a lender, on-line or otherwise, can be worth its weight in gold when you're in a competition to get a house. A seller who knows you've got the money to make the deal is far more likely to pick you, even at a slightly lower price, than another buyer who's got a big "maybe" in front of his or her name when it comes to financing. Check out Chapter 7.

27. *Should I check out the many mortgage Web sites?*

They're easy to find, and they contain a host of information. Also, most have calculators that let you play "what if" games with your monthly payment, down payment, and loan amount. They're a great way not only of getting a mortgage, but of getting immediate information on the current mortgage market. Check out Chapter 7.

28. *Should I not worry about garbage costs?*

Big mistake. These costs can eat you alive. When searching a mortgage Web site, find one that not only tells you the interest rate and points (they all do), but also the incidental costs (garbage fees) for each loan (few do). This will give you a better picture of what you'll actually have to pay. Reread Chapter 7.

29. *Should I apply for a mortgage on-line?*

It's faster, easier, and you can do it in the privacy of your own home. Just be sure you know with whom you're dealing and that it's a major mortgage finance company or lender. Check into Chapter 7.

30. *Should I learn all that I can about mortgages* before *applying?*

Today, mortgage lending is big business in the trillions of dollars per year. Mortgage retailers, with whom you will deal, are working on thin margins, and they want to process you through as quickly as possible. They simply don't have time to educate you from the ground up. So learn as much as you can about mortgages *before* you go after one. See Chapter 8.

31. *Should I use the seller's inspection report?*

Maybe it's legitimate, current, and thorough. Maybe not. Certainly you, as the buyer, never had a chance to go with the inspector to ask questions and learn answers. As a buyer, I always insist on a new inspection report for myself, and you should, too. Check Chapter 9.

32. *Should I look for home inspectors who were old building department inspectors and who belong to professional trade groups?*

It's a good idea. Remember, most inspectors are not yet licensed. You need to check them out thoroughly to be sure they're what they say they are and can perform a good service for you. Be sure to call the references they give you. Check into Chapter 9.

33. *Should I use a bad inspection report to renegotiate the deal?*

You should get the price lowered, repair work done before the sale is completed, or both, if the inspection report reveals damage or defects. Of course, this requires that your sales agreement have an inspection contingency written in. Check with your agent and/or attorney to be sure it's in there and correctly drawn. Check Chapter 9.

34. *Should I just have the overall inspection and let it go at that?*

If the inspector recommends specialty inspections, think seriously about them. It may cost more to have a specialist check out the soil, the structure, or the roof. But, if something is wrong, the few hundred dollars the inspection may cost will pale in comparison to the tens of thousands of dollars it could cost to have the problem remedied. Look into Chapter 9.

35. Should I give serious thought to lead in the home?

In houses built prior to 1978, there's an excellent chance that lead paint was used. If you have small children and they ingest or inhale it, it could cause serious problems. You may want to have the home inspected for lead. Check into Chapter 10.

36. Should I worry about other toxics in the house?

This is a case of what you don't know can hurt you. You don't have to be an alarmist, but it does pay to be careful. I can remember when I was young seeing firemen race into a burning structure wearing just a fireproof jacket. Today's fire personnel would never go into any burning building, including the house you may be considering, without wearing special gas masks to protect them from the toxic fumes. It's something to think about. Check into Chapter 10.

37. Should I check out the water supply?

After all, you'll be drinking from it. You want to watch out for copper and lead in the pipes. And, if the property is fed by well water, you'll want to check for other chemicals, as well as bacteria, in the water. Look into Chapter 10.

38. When buying a condo/co-op, should I look for a Web site?

Not all, of course, but many condominium/cooperatives operate their own Web sites. Usually, it's the home owners' association that puts it up. It can be very helpful and provide much information to the buyer. Check out Chapter 11.

39. Should I watch out for condos/co-ops with high tenant ratios?

Remember, under 10 percent tenants is good. Over 25 percent is bad. There's nothing wrong with renters; however, a preponderance of them in a shared-living facility usually means that some hidden problem exists. Check Chapter 11.

40. *Should I read the CC&Rs and bylaws of the HOA before buying into a shared-living arrangement?*

These are the rules by which you'll have to live. Often, they are strictly enforced. If there's something you can't stand, don't buy into the group. Once you're in, it's very hard (usually impossible) to change the rules. Look into Chapter 11.

41. *Should I beware of high monthly HOA dues?*

If the payments are high, it may indicate a problem, such as a lack of reserves to handle repairs and replacements. Check Chapter 11.

42. *Should I watch out for lawsuits against the HOA?*

A pending lawsuit can make mortgage financing in a condo/co-op very difficult, if not impossible. Also, if the HOA loses the suit, each owner could be assessed to pay for costs, including damages. Look into Chapter 11.

43. *When looking for a new home, should I check out the Internet first?*

Many builders and organizations are there. You may be able to narrow your search considerably before ever leaving your home. Check into Chapter 12.

44. *Should I assume the builder is okay if the house looks okay?*

Check out the builder. It's his or her reputation that you're buying. Find out what else they have built, and then visit the current owners. You'll learn a lot; sometimes, it can be a real eye-opener. Check into Chapter 12.

45. *Should I buy a new home because it will appreciate in value faster?*

Maybe. Then again, maybe not. It depends on location, the market, and what else is available. You have to be just as careful a buyer when purchasing new as when purchasing existing, sometimes more so. See Chapter 12.

46. *Should I be sure the builder has a good warranty?*

It's not that something *might* go wrong. It's that things *will* go wrong, sometimes major things. You want to be assured that the builder, or its insurance company, will cover it all. Check Chapter 12.

47. Should I call the agent, the escrow officer, and the mortgage company before going to the closing?

You'll probably need to bring some documentation with you to the closing. If you don't have it, the deal can't close. Therefore, it's a good idea to check with everyone concerned to find out exactly what you need to bring. Check Chapter 13.

48. Should I watch out for garbage fees?

They are often assessed by both the lender and the escrow company. These days, however, because almost all lenders and escrow companies assess them, they're difficult to avoid. And, it's doubly difficult to try to negotiate them out when you're trying to close the deal. Check into Chapter 13.

49. Should I read the estimate of costs carefully?

The best time to negotiate to have garbage fees removed is when you first contact the lender and are given your estimate of costs. If there's something you don't think is proper, make a big deal about it. If the market's not too hot and there aren't that many loans going through, the lender may just remove it. Check Chapter 13.

50. How Do I Reach Robert Irwin?

Try my Web site, www.robertirwin.com. It includes late breaking information for home buyers and sellers, real estate resources and an e-mail address where you can send questions.

INDEX

ABOUT THE AUTHOR

ROBERT IRWIN, noted real estate broker for more than 30 years, and the author of the best-selling *Tips & Traps* series, serves as a consultant to lenders, investors, and brokers. With over 30 books including *The Pocket Guide for Home Buyers,* Irwin is recognized as one of the most knowledgeable writers in the real estate field.

COMMERCENET is the premier nonprofit organization for promoting and building electronic commerce solutions on the Internet. Visit their Web site at http://www.commerce.net.

E-LOAN is the Internet's largest on-line mortgage service.